SPIRITUAL *Discovery* SERIES

ACTS

TO THE ENDS OF THE EARTH

122582

EMIL BALLIET

Radiant Life

1445 Boonville Avenue
Springfield, MO 65802-1894
02-0212

STAFF

Editor in Chief: Gary Leggett
Series Editor: Clancy Hayes
Assistant Editors: Lori Horne
Gerald Parks
Editorial Assistants: Diane Lamb
Terry Bryant
Design: Steve Lopez
Don Burchfield

Photo Credits:

©1996 PhotoDisc, Inc.: Cover, 1, 3, 4, 5, 24, 68, 82, back cover; Norma Ennis: 38, 54; Cleo Photography: 96; Rick Davis: 32; Gail Denham: 89; David Dobson: 75; Donna Meier: 9; Kumler Photography: 46; Mark Wright, Rockafellow Photography: 61; Jim Whitmer: 16.

Library Of Congress Catalog Card Number: 95-81054
ISBN 0-88243-212-5
Printed in the United States of America

A Study Guide for individual or group study with this book is available
from the Gospel Publishing House (order #02-0112).

Contents

Welcome To The
Spiritual *Discovery* Series

The *Spiritual Discovery Series* is a unique curricula product. It has been designed with today's learner in mind. A quick survey of this guide will reveal many changes from earlier texts. These changes reflect our philosophy of adult education. It is important that you, the teacher/facilitator, understand the reason for the changes and the educational philosophy used to develop the *Spiritual Discovery Series.*

First, you will note interactive questions strategically placed throughout the study guide material. Research reveals that adults want to participate in the process of learning. Too often Sunday School has become a place where students come to hear what the teacher has discovered that week. The *Spiritual Discovery Series* requires individuals to study the Scriptures and make personal discoveries. Not everyone has access to a theological library. With this in mind, our curriculum provides "hard to get" information while leaving the majority of work for the learner.

Second, you will note the only difference between the study guide and the leader's text is the suggested learning methodology. Some may wonder why no additional commentary is provided for the leader. The *Spiritual Discovery Series* places the teacher in the role of facilitator rather than class expert. The teacher/facilitator is seen as a partner in the learning process. The teacher/facilitator should complete the study guide and be prepared to bring his/her personal discoveries to class to be added to the mix. The facilitator's primary function is to keep the class on track and moving. Activities (with approximate time to accomplish them) are provided to reinforce principles and move the class from point to point.

Third, you will note the *Spiritual Discovery Series*' writers do not tell students how to live, but rather point them toward the only Book that has the authority to demand lifestyle reform. Our curriculum is merely a tool leading individuals to the Bible which alone contains definitive answers to life's problems.

The *Spiritual Discovery Series* is an excellent tool for those who wish to engage the minds of their students. You may feel uncomfortable with the change, but in a very short time you will be encouraged by the participation and the level of learning occurring among members of your group.

As always, we at Radiant Life welcome your comments. An evaluation form has been included in this guide. We encourage you to use it. It is our desire to continually improve our products to better meet the needs of those we serve. Thank you for using the *Spiritual Discovery Series*.

USING THE SPIRITUAL DISCOVERY SERIES LEADER'S GUIDE

1 **Study the objective before beginning each session.** It is important that you know what you wish to accomplish before you begin.

---

2 Read through the section entitled "What You Will Need" early enough in the week to **allow time to secure items necessary to direct the session efficiently.** Almost everything you will need to conduct a successful session is provided in the curriculum. Occasionally you will need to provide common items for illustrations. When these are needed, they will be clearly outlined in the "What You Will Need" section.

---

3 "Getting The Group's Attention" is one of the more important parts of the methodology. The leader must **grab the attention of the group from the very beginning.** Be sure to carefully plan this section of the session.

---

4 A transition statement is provided in each study to assist in the logical transition from "Getting The Group's Attention" to the main body of the study. **Reading the transition statement to the group will clearly define the study objective for everyone.**

---

5 **An overhead projector is a valuable communication tool** which is referred to throughout this study. If you do not have access to an overhead projector, write the information on a chalkboard or provide a copy of the overhead master for each group member.

---

6 The methodology used in this study includes discussion, short lectures, study guide responses, prayer, handouts, and brief presentations. Times have been approximated for each method. As the leader, you may **choose to use all of the suggested methods** or select those most useful to you.

---

7 **Provide opportunity for group members to apply principles** discovered in the session.

---

8 **Encourage after-session fellowship.**

General Suggestions To The Group Leader

1 When leading a study group, the leader must **remember the Bible provides the answers and is the authority.** The leader facilitates discovery of biblical truths by the group. Always come prepared to contribute to the discovery process by completing the study guide material beforehand.

---

2 **Begin each session with prayer.** Invite the Holy Spirit to be your guide as you facilitate the discussion.

---

3 **Start on time and finish on time.** Starting late will reinforce tardiness. Finishing late will frustrate those who have made other plans and need to leave. Respect people's time.

---

4 The task of the leader/facilitator is to **keep the group moving and on target.** Avoid tangents. On occasion, the leader may choose to focus large amounts of group time on a particular point of interest, but this should be the exception. The good of the group should not be regularly sacrificed for the individual.

---

5 **Do not allow anyone to dominate the discussion, including yourself.** Encourage participation from those who seldom speak. The group benefits proportionately to the number who participate.

---

6 **Avoid restating or rewording people's answers.** If you think a response is not complete, or not clear to the group, you may wish to ask the group if they have anything to add to the last response.

---

7 **Never put a person on the spot** by asking him to read or pray aloud, without prior arrangement. Ask for volunteers rather than calling on a specific person.

---

8 In most cases, a variety of Bible translations will be present in the group. **Encourage readings from differing translations** to broaden the group's understanding of the text.

---

9 All the study questions are important. However, not all questions will demand an equal amount of group discussion time. Studies have been designed to be completed in 45 to 60 minutes. **Prioritize your time by determining an approximate amount of time to be spent on each activity in advance.**

STUDY 1

THE RISEN CHRIST SPEAKS

Jesus said, "I will build My church." Jesus set in motion God's redemptive reach, through the Church, to the whole world. The Church is commissioned to go into all the world with the good news. The gospel of Christ is the power of God unto salvation. Christ is the living Head of His Body the Church, and the Holy Spirit enables each believer to function as a member of Christ's body.

Scripture discloses the vital links to the life of Christ as revealed in the Gospels and His continuing ministry by the Holy Spirit through the Church. This includes such great themes as the resurrection of Christ and His ascension, teachings concerning the Kingdom, teachings concerning the baptism in the Holy Spirit, and the emphasis on the worldwide missionary plan of evangelism.

Study Objective

To examine the foundation of the Church and develop an appreciation of our spiritual heritage.

What You Will Need

☐ Duplicate enough copies of resource 1A, "Holy Spirit Survey," for each member of the group.
☐ Prepare a report on Theophilus, the recipient of the Gospel of Luke and the Book of Acts.
☐ Overhead projector.
☐ Prepare an overhead transparency of resource 1B, "The First Missionaries."
☐ Prepare a sign-up sheet for group members to sign up to bring refreshments for subsequent sessions.
☐ Refreshments for group fellowship following the session.

Getting The Group's Attention

(All times are estimates. 6 minutes)

Begin by having group members identify themselves. Keep this informal by asking for names and where they grew up.

Following the introductions, distribute resource 1A, "Holy Spirit Survey," to each group member. After the group has completed the survey, ask individuals to share their responses to item 5 on the work sheet.

The resurrection of Jesus and the coming of the Holy Spirit provide the foundation for the Church that Christ is building.

Transition Statement

Lecture
(5 minutes)
Present the report on Theophilus which you prepared. Use information discovered in study guide items 1-3 to assist your lecture. Allow time for discussion after the presentation.

Response
(5 minutes)
Have group members discuss their responses to study guide item 4 and also how they think they would have reacted if they had found themselves in the same situation.

Discussion
(4 minutes)
Ask individuals to explain how Jesus' resurrection sets Christianity apart from other religions.

1. According to Acts 1:1, who is the original recipient of the Book of Acts?

____

2. Compare Luke 1:1-4 with Acts 1:1-3. Based on the similarities and information given in these verses, who is the author of the Book of Acts?

____

3. Read Acts 1:1-3. What are we told about Jesus in these three verses?

____

____

____

4. Record the initial reactions to Jesus' resurrection in each of the following situations.

Luke 24:1-12 ____

____

Luke 24:13-32 _______________________________________

____

Luke 24:36-43 _______________________________________

____

John 20:11-18 _______________________________________

____

John 20:26-31 _______________________________________

____

There are but three possible explanations of Jesus' empty tomb: (1) Jesus' enemies stole His body from the tomb; (2) His disciples removed His body; or (3) Jesus rose from the dead as He said He would. If Jesus' enemies had stolen His body from the tomb, they had in their possession a weapon lethal enough to have destroyed Christianity. Why didn't they display the body? On the Day of Pentecost, Peter charged the religious authorities with having killed the Prince of Glory. In the same breath Peter declared that God had raised Jesus from the dead. If His enemies could have produced the body of Jesus, Peter and the disciples could have been booed and hissed out of Jerusalem. Christianity would have died at the hour of its birth. Jesus' enemies would have liked to accomplish this. They didn't do it; they couldn't do it, because they did not have the body of Jesus in their possession.

Did Jesus' disciples remove His body from the tomb? To assert this is the equivalent of saying that the disciples built the Church on a doctrine they knew to be a lie. And when they preached the resurrection of Christ, they were deliberately proclaiming a falsehood. The record of history is this: all but one of the apostles died as martyrs because of the gospel they preached. Can you believe that without exception, quietly, uncomplainingly, triumphantly, each one would die in witness to a lie? This is preposterous!

This leaves only the third possibility—the tomb was empty because Christ rose from the dead as He said He would. And this is the foundation on which Christianity rests. We believe in the living, victorious Christ of the resurrection.

On the day of His resurrection, Jesus revealed himself to Mary Magdalene, to Simon Peter, and to Cleopas and his companion as they walked toward Emmaus.

✎ **5. To what did Jesus point to clarify His death and resurrection? (Luke 24:25-27, 44-46).**

____

____

____

____

Jesus' resurrection was the divine demonstration of His deity and the triumph of His redemptive work.

✎ **6. What further evidence does 1 Corinthians 15:3-8 offer for the fact of the resurrection of Christ?**

____

____

____

____

____

____

Response
(3 minutes)
Have group members share their responses to study guide item 6.

The apostles saw Jesus and fellowshipped with Him after His mighty triumph over death. To them, it was not a matter of dogma or doctrine. Jesus, their living Lord, moved among them for 40 days after His resurrection. They saw Him; they knew Him; and their faith rested on indisputable fact.

The infallible, convincing proofs of Christ's resurrection have withstood the test of 2,000 years of time. As Lyman Abbot declared, "The resurrection of Jesus Christ is the best-attested fact of history." Our service, therefore, is not to a dead leader. We serve a living Lord!

THE RENEWED DISCIPLES

The post-resurrection appearances of Jesus had an electrifying effect upon the disciples.

✎ **7. Read Acts 1:6. What did the disciples anticipate as a result of Christ's resurrection?**

____

____

Response
(2 minutes)
Have individuals share their responses to study guide item 7.

Carefully note that Jesus did not rebuke the disciples. Rather, He gave them clearer light on the sequence of events which must precede the millennial reign of Messiah. During the 40 days in which He revealed himself, Jesus patiently guided the disciples into an understanding of the divine plan as outlined in the Scriptures.

The disciples' concept of Jesus was changed and vastly enlarged. Prior to Calvary they saw in Him the hope for the fulfillment of the national dream of a revitalized, independent Israel. Now they were beginning to grasp the meaning of the commission to witness, to preach repentance and remission of sins among all nations, beginning at Jerusalem.

Testimony
(4 minutes)
Ask individuals to share their response the first time they heard about Calvary and the Resurrection.

8. Read Acts 1:8. According to this passage, who is responsible for revitalizing Israel and beyond? Explain how this is to occur.

____

____

____

The death and resurrection of Jesus were like key pieces in a puzzle. With these key pieces, the picture of redemption became a beautiful, completed whole. They realized that the Jesus whom they loved and followed in those pre-Calvary days had been limited, localized. He could be in only one place at a time. But now, the risen Christ by His Holy Spirit through His spiritual Body, the Church, could minister to the world.

9. Read Acts 1:4-26. List the various activities the disciples engaged in during the period between Jesus' ascension and the Day of Pentecost.

____

____

____

This passage of Scripture (Acts 1:4-26) provides us with our final glimpse of the disciples before Pentecost. It is a challenging and instructive picture. The disciples were bound together in a remarkable unity of faith and love. Calvary had scattered them, but the Resurrection reunited them. Now they were welded together in closer ties than ever through their risen Lord. With clarity and authority they quoted the messianic psalms (Psalms 41; 69; 109) and applied them as fulfilled prophecies concerning Judas and Christ.

From our human point of view it would seem to us that the disciples were admirably prepared to go to the world as witnesses for Christ. They knew the reality of the risen Lord in a deep, personal sense. They had been taught in the Scriptures by Jesus himself. He had painstakingly unfolded before them the grand panorama of redemption. Wasn't this sufficient?

Quite clearly, Jesus did not believe that they were sufficiently prepared. He knew that they needed the Person and the gifts of the Holy Spirit. And He instructed them not to begin their mission until they received power from on high. He well knew the importance of the power of the Holy Spirit. Only in the energy of the Spirit could the gospel be carried successfully to the world. This is the reason He commanded them to wait for the outpouring of the Holy Spirit.

THE HOLY SPIRIT

In obedience to Christ's command, the disciples gathered in an upper room to wait for the promise of the Father. [Note that *the promise of the Father*, *the promised Holy Spirit*, and *the baptism in the Holy Spirit* are synonymous terms.]

Before His crucifixion, Jesus taught very explicitly about the coming ministry of the Holy Spirit.

10. Read John 14:16. Imagine that you know nothing about the Holy Spirit. How would you interpret what Jesus was saying in this verse of Scripture?

____

____

____

Jesus used the word *Paraclete* to describe the relationship of the Spirit to the disciples. No one English word can fully convey the meaning of *Paraclete*. The full scope of the word means "one called alongside to help, an advocate, one who pleads the cause of another, a representative acting in behalf of another."

The absolute necessity of the presence and ministry of the Holy Spirit in and through the believer is easy to grasp. The same Holy Spirit who anointed and ministered through Christ is now to come and indwell each believer. And His indwelling will be to the believer the source and the secret of all power in working and witnessing. The Spirit-filled believer moves in the stream of the ministry of the Holy Spirit. And what is the ministry of the Holy Spirit? He guides into all truth, testifies to Christ, takes of the things of Christ and reveals them to others. He speaks and ministers with the same compassion and power as Jesus would have ministered were He present in person.

The truth of the personal being of the Holy Spirit is immensely important because in this fact lies the secret and the purpose of the baptism in the Holy Spirit. The Holy Spirit is not an invisible force which we grasp and use. The Holy Spirit is a living Person who grasps and uses us!

The Day of Pentecost was a particularly appropriate time for the coming of the Holy Spirit. First, it was called the "day of the firstfruits" (Numbers 28:26). The firstfruits of the Church (3,000 souls) were the promise of an ever-increasing harvest to be reaped throughout the world. Secondly, it was a time when Israelites were to remember that they had been bondslaves in Egypt, but God had set them free (Deuteronomy 16:12). How fitting that, on this day, the Spirit came to empower the Church to proclaim the message that makes people free. Finally, Jews had gathered in Jerusalem from all over the world. What a strategic time for the Church, with its worldwide commission, to begin its ministry.

What is the baptism in the Holy Spirit? It is just exactly what the word *baptism* implies—it is a complete immersion of one's spirit, soul, and body in the Holy Spirit.

11. To what does Jesus compare the baptism in the Holy Spirit in Acts 1:4,5?

____

This was the only illustration the Lord Jesus gave concerning this baptism in the Holy Spirit. In Matthew 3:11 John alludes to this comparison. The baptism in the Holy Spirit was the normal experience of all in the Early Church. This experience is distinct from, and subsequent to, the experience of the new birth.

12. Read Acts 8:12-17; 10:30-46; 19:1-6. What had the people in each of these examples experienced before they were baptized in the Holy Spirit?

____

13. Read Acts 2:2-4. List the signs which accompanied the coming of the Holy Spirit on the Day of Pentecost.

____

____

____

The signs accompanying the Holy Spirit's outpouring were awesome. They spoke of the irresistible power, intense energy, and glowing light of the Holy Spirit and were reminiscent of the burning bush that Moses saw. First, the Holy Spirit filled the room and then each person. Here also began the mysterious, glorious experience of magnifying God in languages prompted by the Holy Spirit.

Were there not other signs on the Day of Pentecost? There were. But this is the one sign which God repeated in each instance in which individuals received the baptism in the Spirit. Is it possible to receive the baptism in the Holy Spirit without speaking in tongues? It is fruitless to argue this question because everyone who received the Baptism in the Scripture, and an evidence was recorded, did speak with other tongues.

Ask group members, "Why is it important to have an initial physical evidence of the baptism in the Holy Spirit?"

Ask group members, "Why is Peter's statement in Acts 11:17 important to belief in the baptism in the Holy Spirit for today?"

14. Look at the five outpourings of the Spirit recorded in the Book of Acts: 2:2-4; 8:17; 9:17; 10:44; and 19:6. What evidence of the baptism in the Holy Spirit is most often recorded in these instances?

____

____

Read 1 Corinthians 14:18. According to this passage of Scripture, what was Paul's experience with the phenomenon commonly called "speaking in tongues"?

____

____

____

Without a doubt, Paul began speaking in tongues the same time any other person who is baptized in the Holy Spirit begins to speak in tongues—right at the time he received the Baptism! There is no evidence in the Scriptures to indicate that anyone ever began to speak in tongues except as he or she received the baptism in the Holy Spirit. What about the Samaritan believers? Follow the story thread carefully and you will discover the strong inference that the same supernatural evidence of the Baptism witnessed elsewhere was witnessed there also.

The promise of the Holy Spirit is relevant for believers now. At Pentecost a pattern was provided for all who would receive the Spirit. There is a highly important phrase employed by the apostle Peter as he reported the outpouring of the Holy Spirit on the Gentiles at Caesarea in Acts 11. He stated to the brethren in Jerusalem that the baptism in the Holy Spirit given to the Gentiles at Caesarea was the same as the Baptism they had received at Pentecost.

15. Read Joel 2:28-32 and then Acts 2:16-21. What significance do these verses have for us today?

____

____

____

____

It is essential that those who receive the baptism in the Holy Spirit today be able to scripturally describe their experience by pointing back to the Day of Pentecost and saying with the apostle Peter that it is what was spoken by the prophet Joel. The Holy Spirit comes now, as then, to those willing to receive Him.

SUMMARY

The first chapter of Acts is very important to our understanding of the development of the Early Church. It serves as an informative connection between the end of Jesus' ministry on earth and the beginning of the Church. Many of the things Christ spoke about prior to His death and resurrection are clarified and confirmed both to His disciples and to us.

Just as Jesus had promised, the Holy Spirit was sent to a group of believers who were obediently waiting in faith. This historic event serves as a foundation to the ministry of the New Testament Church and the Church's ministry in the present age until the Lord returns.

Let's pray that the anointing and illumination that only the Holy Spirit can give will be ours as we continue with our study into the birth and infancy of the Church.

LET'S REVIEW

✎ **1. What evidence points to Luke as the author of both the Gospel of Luke and the Book of Acts?**

____

____

____

✎ **2. What are some of the strong evidences for the resurrection of Jesus from the dead?**

____

____

____

____

____

✎ **3. What is the primary purpose of the baptism in the Spirit?**

____

____

____

____

____

✎ **4. Why was the Holy Spirit given at Pentecost?**

____

____

____

____

✎ **5. What is the promise and purpose of the Holy Spirit for today's Church?**

____

____

____

____

____

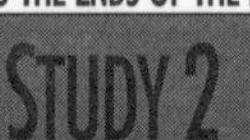

STUDY 2

To study the initial acts of the apostles following their Baptism and embrace their behavior as a model for our lives.

✓ **What You Will Need**

☐ Duplicate enough copies of resources 2A, "The Miracles Of The Apostles," and 2B, "How Can We Witness?" for each group member.

☐ Reports of current outpourings of revival (i.e., magazine articles, newspaper clippings, letters).

Getting The Group's Attention

(All times are estimates. 5 minutes)

Ask group members the following questions:

1. "What first comes to mind when you hear the term *D day*?"

2. "How could the Day of Pentecost be compared to a D day?"

3. "Which soldier has more will to win: one who has been hired or one who is fighting for his or her homeland and family?"

4. "As soldiers in Christ's army, how is our motivation for witnessing similar to that of the soldier defending home and country?"

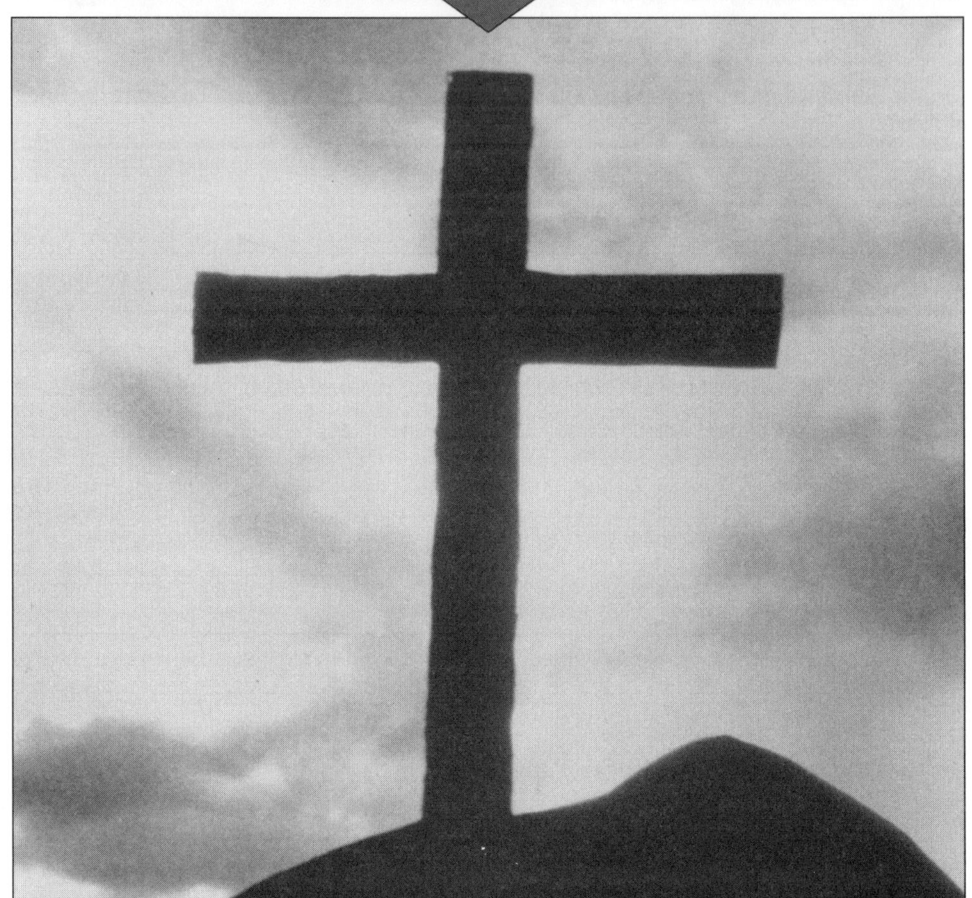

THE DYNAMIC WITNESS

The Day of Pentecost was *D day* in the divine strategy for worldwide evangelism. Christ's resurrection fully established His authority as Son of God and Messiah. He then spent 40 days with His rejoicing followers to ground them thoroughly in the Scriptures concerning redemption. The Pentecostal experience launched the Church with a dynamic thrust.

The effectiveness of this strategy appeared in the preaching of the apostles and deacons as recorded in Acts. They quoted the Scriptures with great confidence and authority. They interpreted the meaning of the prophecies with clarity and finality.

Clothed with the power of the Holy Spirit, the Church began its witness with deep, moving commitment to Christ and to each other.

Transition Statement ➡ The acts of the apostles witnessed to the resurrection power of Christ.

WITNESS THROUGH PREACHING

Before Pentecost, Jesus' followers seemed scarcely more than a loosely grouped gathering of wondering, learning disciples. They had studied the Scriptures from childhood. They had committed entire segments of the Bible to memory under the tutelage of the rabbis. But for 40 days following the Resurrection, they were guided by Jesus into the spiritual insights of the continuous revelation of redemption found in Moses, the Prophets, and the Psalms (Luke 24:44). They were familiar with these commonly accepted divisions of the Scriptures: "Moses" meant the Pentateuch, "the Prophets" included the prophetic and historical writings, and "the Psalms" encompassed the devotional, poetic books. Thus, the entire Bible was seen to present one comprehensive, cohesive statement of the divine plan of Redemption.

Following the Pentecostal baptism, the disciples were transformed into flaming heralds. Christ, their Lord, had returned to the Father. And now, commissioned and baptized in the Holy Spirit, they were ready to begin the great assignment of witnessing to the world. The enabling power of the Holy Spirit baptism clothed their witness with dynamic effectiveness.

The powerful ministry of the disciples at Pentecost focused on the major points of the gospel: the redemptive meaning of the death and the resurrection of Jesus, the sovereignty of God, the call to repentance, and the promise of the forgiveness of sin.

1. Read Acts 2:5-7. What is significant about the setting for the initial outpouring of the Holy Spirit?

____

____

____

To the utter amazement of the visitors, here were Jews speaking the praises of God in the languages of the nations from which they had come. And the astonishing thing was that the disciples were speaking those foreign languages with the discernible accents of Galileans.

Peter, as spokesman for the apostolic band, addressed the multitude, not in tongues, but in the common language of the people. His sermon is a beautiful example of Spirit-anointed witnessing through preaching.

2. From reading Acts 2:2-16,33, what influenced Peter to stand up and respond to the crowd?

____

____

3. Read Acts 2:7-13. What three questions were voiced by the crowd?

____

____

____

____

4. In Acts 2:15, how did Peter respond to the crowd's accusation of drunkenness?

____

____

Lecture
(2 minutes)
Summarize the first few paragraphs under the heading "Witness Through Preaching" from the parallel column.

Response
(2 minutes)
Have individuals share their responses to study guide item 2.

Response
(2 minutes)
Have group members share their responses to study guide item 3.

Discussion
(3 minutes)

Ask group members the following questions:

1. "Why was Peter's preaching style so effective?"

2. "How can this method be used in personal witnessing?"

Response
(4 minutes)

Have group members share their responses to study guide item 6. Ask, "What lesson can we learn from Peter's life and ministry?"

Have a volunteer read 1 Corinthians 1:27-29 to emphasize whom Christ can use as witnesses.

Response
(2 minutes)

Have individuals share their responses to study guide item 8.

Peter's sermon was direct and simple. He took the words of the crowd's inquiry and repeated them three times in the course of his reply. Peter's answer was clear. Any child in the crowd could have followed his words with understanding.

The third hour of the day (or 9 a.m.) was the hour of sacrifice, and faithful believers in Israel neither ate nor drank until that hour.

Peter, inspired by the Spirit, employed a sound principle of educational psychology. He used the known to lead into the unknown. First, he quoted the prophet Joel. And then he explained that the Jesus who was crucified and risen again is the One who fulfilled Joel's prophecy by pouring out the Holy Spirit.

5. Read Acts 2:22-28. List the facts Peter used to establish Jesus' credibility.

____

____

____

____

____

6. Compare Matthew 26:69-75 and Peter's sermon in Acts 2:14-39. How has Peter's approach to confrontation changed?

____

How much time had elapsed between the two incidents?

____

What would account for this sudden change?

____

Peter's sermon was filled with Scripture quotations. First, he cited Joel 2:28-32. It is a description of the future of the Church. This passage begins with God's promise to pour out His Spirit on all people. It then identifies the spiritual gifts of the people. The climaxing end of the age is depicted with the prophecy to show wonders in the heavens and on the earth.

7. Look up Psalms 16:8-11 and 110:1, two passages of Scripture that Peter quotes in his sermon. Whom is David referring to here?

____

Again, Peter quoted the prophetic words of David to support the witness to Jesus' resurrection. He made it clear that David could not have spoken of himself when he spoke of God not allowing the Holy One to decay (Psalm 16:10). David's tomb was, and is to this day, a well-known shrine in Jerusalem. The resurrection of Jesus, David's greater Son, fulfilled this prophecy.

Also, Peter referred to the prophetic statements in Psalm 110:1. David, he said, is not ascended into heaven, but Jesus is. The mystery and the glory of the Pentecostal outpouring is positive proof of Jesus' ascension. The fulfillment of these prophetic Scriptures served to identify the true person of Jesus—He is both Lord and Messiah.

Finally, Peter preached for a result—and got it!

8. According to Acts 2:41, what was the result of Peter's sermon?

____

ACTS: TO THE ENDS OF THE EARTH, LEADER'S GUIDE

WITNESS THROUGH BAPTISM

The amazing power of the Pentecostal witness was evidenced by the amazing response. Suddenly, a church was born! When the Day of Pentecost began, there was but a handful of disciples. But when the day ended, their numbers had been increased tremendously.

✎ **9. Read Acts 8:26-39 and Acts 16:30-33. What was the normal practice after someone became saved?**

____

Repentance brought forgiveness, and forgiveness called for a demonstration of that new state. It must be remembered that the 3,000 saved on the Day of Pentecost were not baptized in order to be saved. They were baptized because they were saved. And now, by the act of baptism, they were identified with Jesus in His death, burial, and resurrection (Romans 6:3-6). And each baptism became a witness to the crucified, entombed, and risen Savior.

It remains a normal and proper part of Christian experience for baptism to follow repentance and faith.

WITNESS THROUGH FELLOWSHIP

A dynamic new fellowship was created by the outpouring of the Holy Spirit. It became a forceful witness to Jerusalem because it glowed with love. No sacrifice was considered too great in meeting the needs of brothers and sisters in Christ. Some have called this a Christian form of communism. But communism was never like this. The only compulsion in this fellowship was love. The true worth of each individual was seen in the light of the Cross, and the Resurrection—and now, in the light of the outpoured Spirit. There were no superiors and no inferiors in this fellowship. All were one in Christ.

✎ **10. Read Acts 2:42-46. Describe the atmosphere and attitude surrounding the newly born Church.**

____

____

____

What aspects of the description just given would you like to see evidenced in the Church today?

____

____

What could you do to make this a reality?

____

____

____

These apostolic believers were gripped with a dynamic new fellowship. It encompassed their whole lives—spiritually, materially, physically—and it thoroughly pervaded their home life. This thrilling new fellowship had a mighty impact on the city of Jerusalem (Acts 2:43).

Jerusalem was buzzing with the happenings at Pentecost. The quiet followers of Jesus were now fiery, forceful witnesses. New disciples were being added daily. And the promised power of the Holy Spirit now moved them into deeper dimensions of service.

11. Compare Luke 5:17-26 with Acts 3:1-8. How are these accounts similar?

____

____

What do these similarities reveal about the ministry of the Spirit-filled disciples?

____

____

The disciples were beginning to grasp the fact that the Holy Spirit would minister through them, just as Jesus would have ministered were He present in the flesh. Witnessing took on new meaning as Peter and John ministered to the lame man at the gate of the temple. This remarkable healing opened new and wonderful opportunities to preach the good news about their risen Lord.

The deep-rooted relationship between the Old and the New Testaments is illustrated in the fact that Peter and John and the early disciples went daily to the temple for prayer. The temple continued to be their sanctuary, for Judaism and Christianity grew out of the promises of God concerning the Redeemer, and the temple was dedicated to the mighty God who had given the promises.

The helpless man at the gate was a familiar figure to all who came to the temple. Sitting at the entrance to the temple dedicated to the living God, he presents a picture of helpless humanity in its deepest need. Peter and John, filled with the Spirit, were in the conscious possession of the power of God and used it to minister to this man.

12. What promise did the events of Acts 3:1-8 fulfill? (Mark 16:20).

____

____

13. Read Acts 3:11-26. How did Peter respond to the crowd's reaction to this healing, and what did he take the opportunity to do while he had that crowd assembled?

____

____

Peter's opening words were filled with thrilling meaning. He ascribed the miracle to "the God of Abraham, and of Isaac, and of Jacob, the God of our fathers." In effect, he said, Abraham would have forever remained in obscurity and heathenism, but for the God of miracles. There would not have been a son called Isaac were it not for the miracle power of God. It was God who changed the deceiving, crooked Jacob into Israel. And were it not for the miracle power of God there would not be a nation called Israel. Our God is the God of miracles!

And then Peter entered into a bold proclamation of the gospel. The God of miracles gave His Son Jesus. And though the people had clamored that Jesus be crucified, God raised Him from the dead. The miracle of healing was evidence of the power of the risen Lord. And in the light of this positive evidence Peter called on all to repent.

Sidebar (left column):

Response
(3 minutes)

Have individuals share their responses to study guide item 11. After responses have been given ask, "What directive does your response give you concerning your ministry potential?"

Handout
(3 minutes)

Distribute a copy of resource 2A, "The Miracles Of The Apostles," to each individual. Allow group members time to complete it so they have an idea of the miracles performed after Jesus' ascension.

Read
(2 minutes)

Have a volunteer read Mark 16:20 and John 14:12,13 to help illustrate Jesus' promise for signs following.

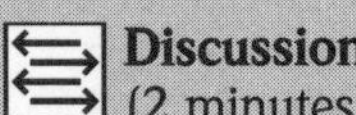

Discussion
(2 minutes)

Ask group members, "Why do you think miracles seem to occur more in some locations than others?"

✎ **14. In your opinion, why do miracles provide such an effective means of leading people to Christ?**

____

____

____

____

WITNESS THROUGH ASSURANCE

The healing of the lame man created a storm of opposition. It brought the disciples into a direct doctrinal conflict with the Sadducees. Peter proclaimed the resurrection of Jesus and attributed this healing to the power of the risen Christ.

✎ **15. Read Acts 4:1-3. What seemed to be the point of contention between Peter and John and the Sadducees?**

____

____

How does this reveal the truth of Jesus' words recorded in Matthew 15:9?

____

____

The temple police, under orders from the Sadducees, arrested the apostles and put them in jail. But the apostles saw their trial before the Sanhedrin as a choice opportunity to witness for their Lord. Jesus had been in conflict with the Sadducees. He had charged that the Sadducees had corrupted the truth of the Word of God by their liberal theology, teaching as doctrine the rules of humans. Peter and John faced the same court—an ecclesiastical court of cold, proud religionists. The judges took no joy in the healing of the lame man. They arrogantly asked Peter and John by what authority they had performed this act.

✎ **16. What was Peter's answer to the Sadducees' question? (Acts 4:9,10).**

____

____

It may have been the Sadducees' hope that anger and a ruthless show of authority would intimidate the apostles. But Peter, freshly filled with the Spirit, answered with great courage. The Jesus whom they had rejected had been raised from death by God, and His resurrection proclaimed Him to be the chief cornerstone in God's temple of redemption.

✎ **17. How did the Sanhedrin answer Peter's anointed defense of their charges? (Acts 4:13-22).**

____

____

____

Response
(2 minutes)
Have individuals share their responses to study guide item 17.

____

____

____

The Sanhedrin seemed completely frustrated. Here were ordinary men addressing them with extraordinary power. Even more frustrating was the presence of the healed man. He stood with the apostles, either having been jailed with them, or having gotten there early in the morning for the trial. The reality of his healing was undeniable and offered solid substance to the witness concerning Jesus and His resurrection.

The discussion of the Sanhedrin presents a pitiful scene—religious leaders blinded by unbelief, prejudice, and anger. So much so that they deliberately closed their eyes to the indisputable evidence before them. Their only concern was how to stop the witness of Jesus' disciples.

But the Sanhedrin were thwarted in their attempts. The disciples were courageous in their conviction. For them the principle was clear—if what they believed was right, they must speak. They were totally convinced of the deity of Jesus and therefore His right to command their obedience. They could not be silent when He commanded them to speak.

The attempt at intimidation failed. The Sanhedrin could not frighten the disciples into submission. After further threats, they were forced to let Peter and John go. Fear restrained the Sanhedrin from further action. Being released, the apostles returned to their own company and reported the events of the hearing.

18. According to Acts 4:23-37, how did the new Christians react when Peter and John returned?

____

____

What was the result?

____

____

____

SUMMARY

Those who knew the believers (and especially the apostles) prior to the Day of Pentecost must certainly have been astonished at the transformation that the power of the Holy Spirit had accomplished. What had been a weak and disorganized group of people, now became strengthened in fellowship and courageous in witness for their ascended Lord.

This powerful witness demonstrated itself in many ways. The apostles' preaching, the new converts' visible identification with Jesus in water baptism, the bonding in love of the growing fellowship of believers, and the miraculous power evident through the apostles' ministry in the name of Jesus were signs that even the most ferocious of opponents could not deny. One of the most descriptive evidences in all of the Bible of the difference the Holy Spirit makes comes from the Sanhedrin. When they saw the courage of Peter and John, ordinary and uneducated, they were amazed and had to acknowledge that these men had been with Jesus.

The power of the Holy Spirit is the only explanation for the new boldness demonstrated by the disciples. Jesus knew they could not carry out their evangelism task without this power. The same is true for us today. When we allow the Holy Spirit to work through us, we will have a fresh courage to declare the message of redemption provided by Jesus in His death and resurrection. We will have a confidence to fulfill Christ's command to preach the gospel to all the world.

Discussion
(4 minutes)

Ask group members the following questions:

1. "What is the difference between religion and Christianity?"

2. "What is the danger of not accepting the truths of God?"

Presentation
(4 minutes)

Read the reports of revival which you brought to the session. Allow individuals to look at them and make comments on the revival power of God in the world today.

Small Groups
(5 minutes)

Have the larger group form groups of 3 or 4 individuals. Distribute resource 2B, "How Can We Witness?" Have the group discuss the various ways of reaching others for Christ.

Have the small groups stay intact for the closing prayer time.

LET'S REVIEW

1. What basic truths did Peter emphasize in his sermons?

____

____

____

2. What did Peter share with the lame man?

____

____

3. Name the three titles Peter ascribes to Jesus.

____

____

____

4. Why were the Sadducees upset with Peter's preaching?

____

____

____

5. What unanswerable evidence supported Peter before the Sanhedrin?

____

____

____

6. How can we begin to witness with the boldness of Peter?

____

____

____

Review
(3 minutes)

Select two or three items from the "Let's Review" section to review the study.

Closing Prayer
(2 minutes)

Close with prayer asking God to work through group members, with the power of His Holy Spirit, to do great things for His glory.

Preparing For Next Session

Remind individuals to complete study 3 before the next session.

Group Fellowship
(5 minutes)

Encourage group members to share together in fellowship and refreshments.

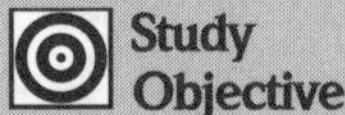

Study Objective

To observe the fledgling Church's reaction to difficult situations and determine to follow its example when facing struggles in our lives.

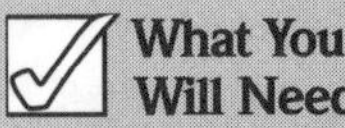

What You Will Need

☐ Marker board markers.
☐ Reports from around the world of attacks on the Church.
☐ Duplicate enough copies of resource 3A, "Saddu-who?" for each group member. You may wish to put these two pages back-to-back when making copies.

Getting The Group's Attention

(All times are estimates. 7 minutes)

Have group members share ways the Church around the world is being attacked today (both within and without). Ask an individual to write responses on the marker board as the group calls out examples.

Share the reports you brought to the session and be sure to point out such things as mediocrity and hypocrisy as well.

Have group members pray over the items listed and for more boldness, when faced with personal persecution.

THE CHURCH UNDER FIRE

The Early Church moved forward with irresistible power. Their numbers increased dramatically. It was inevitable that the Apostolic Church would be tested by fiery trials. And the fiery testing was not long in coming. The Sanhedrin, the Sadducees in particular, threatened them for preaching in the name of Jesus. This served only to deepen the apostles' fervor and determination. They responded to threats with a truly remarkable prayer meeting in Acts 4. The burden of their prayer was not for protection, but for greater boldness in speaking the Word. They prayed that more and greater signs might be done in the name of Jesus.

The unity of the Church was threatened from within by deceit and dissension and from without by the threat of martyrdom. The result of these trials demonstrated God's faithfulness to His followers and to His plan.

Transition Statement

We can stand firm when faced with threats and persecution.

THREATENED BY DECEIT

The fellowship of the Jerusalem Church was a beautiful thing. There was an overwhelming sense of the presence of the Lord Jesus Christ which bound the believers together as one. They shared a fellowship of faith and a concern for each other.

1. Read Acts 4:32-37. What characteristic do we see in the Early Church from its beginning?

____

____

Whatever could succeed in destroying the unity of that fellowship would destroy the Church. Thus, the temptation to hypocrisy was the most subtle, the most dangerous, attack launched against the Church.

It was against this background of inspiring fellowship that the first serious threat to the Church's unity came.

2. Studying Acts 5:1-4, what was the terrible sin that Ananias and Sapphira committed?

____

____

Ananias and Sapphira's sin must be studied in the light of the context. Luke ends the fourth chapter of Acts with the account of Barnabas' donation. In the fifth chapter Luke begins by contrasting Ananias and Barnabas. Barnabas gave a gift prompted by love. Ananias also gave a gift, but his motivation was quite different.

Ananias' sin did not consist in keeping back part of the price of the property he had sold. He had a perfect right to retain part or all of the money for himself. Simply stated, Ananias wanted the honor and the blessing that had come to Barnabas but he did not want to pay the same price.

3. According to Acts 5:3, who was the source of Ananias' sin?

____

This attack was directed at the very thing that had excited the admiration and respect of the people of Jerusalem—the concern the disciples showed for each other. In essence, the devilish scheme was this—pretend something which is not true.

Satan failed to stop the Church by intimidation and threats. Now, he proposed to destroy it from within by seducing its members. But there was a great searcher of hearts in the Church—the Holy Spirit. Note Peter's question to Ananias regarding Satan filling his heart. The devil cannot gain entrance into our lives unless we let him.

4. Look up James 4:7 and 1 John 4:4. Record the assurances that we are given in these verses.

____

____

____

____

There was no excuse for the sin committed by Ananias and Sapphira. No one was asked to sell property and give the money to the apostles for distribution. Ananias and Sapphira may have thought that they were deceiving Peter and the rest of the Church,

Lecture
(5 minutes)

Present the material under the heading, "Threatened By Deceit." Select various study guide response items to supplement your lecture.

but they failed to realize that the real leader of the Church is the omniscient Holy Spirit. Peter, as the mouthpiece of the Spirit, exposed the sin which had been supernaturally revealed to him, and judgment fell on both Ananias and Sapphira.

5. Read Acts 5:7-10. What evidence is there that this sin was premeditated?

____

____

How might this fact help explain the severity of the sentence Ananias and Sapphira received?

____

____

____

It was a severe judgment which had a jolting impact on the Church as well as upon those outside the Church. For those within the Church the message was clear. God is a holy God! And those who walk with Him must be honest and transparent in their relationship with Him. It taught the people on the outside that the Church was a holy fellowship where no dishonesty would be tolerated. Naturally, unless a person really meant business, he would hesitate to join a church where hypocrites were struck dead.

6. From Acts 5:11-16, what feelings did the people have towards the Church after the incident involving Ananias and Sapphira?

____

____

What was the spiritual result?

____

____

____

THREATENED BY PRESSURE

Revival fires flamed through Jerusalem. Multitudes poured into the city with their sick and they were healed. The clash with the ecclesiastical authorities now blazed into the open. In their wrath, they ordered the apostles arrested and confined in the common prison. Notice was sent to all the members of the Sanhedrin to come to a special meeting the following morning.

7. Read Acts 5:17,18. What motivated the Sadducees to arrest the apostles?

____

8. Read Acts 5:19-21. How did God intervene on behalf of the apostles?

____

____

Discussion
(5 minutes)

Ask the following questions:

1. "One child accidentally bumps into a lamp and breaks it and another picks up a lamp and purposely smashes it to the ground, how should each child be dealt with?"

2. "Why was there a difference in your approach?"

3. "How does this 'parenting principle' help explain the account of Ananias and Sapphira?"

Discussion
(4 minutes)

Ask group members the following questions:

1. "How does the world view the Church today?"

2. "How can the Church present a firm message of biblical principles to the world and yet show love and concern for believers?"

Response
(3 minutes)

Have individuals share their responses to study guide items 7 and 8.

What were they told to do?

____

____

____

The full gathering of the Sanhedrin met at the time appointed, but when the captain was ordered to produce the prisoners, he was forced to report that the cells were empty. Then came the message that the apostles were back in the temple preaching to the people. It is significant that the temple police regarded the apostles with new respect and brought them without violence.

9. What were some of the beliefs of the Sadducees which set them apart from other groups and produced conflict with the disciples? (Acts 23:8).

____

____

There must have been a sharp sense of exasperation or frustration on the part of the Sadducees. For the Sadducees, as the liberalists in religion, insisted that these things proclaimed by the apostles were figments of imagination. They could not be! And yet, here were the apostles insisting that their Lord was risen from the dead, that an angel had set them free from the prison, and that in obedience to the angel's command, they had returned to the temple to preach. It was too much! The Sanhedrin asked no questions about their remarkable escape. In a surprising admission, the Sanhedrin charged that the apostles had impacted Jerusalem (Acts 5:28).

10. Read Acts 5:29. On what basis did Peter make his remark?

____

____

Peter's reply was clear and boldly courageous. He restated the one great principle which governed the lives of the disciples—we must obey God. The fisherman's words cut deeply and stirred murderous feelings in the Sadducees.

11. Read Acts 5:34-40. What argument did Gamaliel use to calm down the Sanhedrin?

____

____

The Sadducees reluctantly agreed. They ordered the apostles beaten, commanded them to cease preaching in the name of Jesus, and released them. But the apostles, true to their Lord, did not stop teaching and preaching about Jesus Christ. The threat of ecclesiastical pressure did not intimidate them.

12. Persecution often causes groups and individuals to hold more strongly to their beliefs. Why is this the case? (Acts 5:40-42).

____

____

Handout
(6 minutes)
Distribute the copies of resource 3A, "Saddu-who?" to each member of the group. Lead the group in reading through the contrast and comparison of the two leading Jewish religious groups of that time.

Response
(2 minutes)
Have group members share their responses to study guide item 11.

Response
(3 minutes)
Have individuals share their responses to study guide item 12.

THREATENED BY DISSENSION

Thus far, the infant Church had been subjected to the pressure of official animosity and tested within by attempted deceit. Yet another serious problem threatened the unity of the Church—dissension.

13. According to Acts 6:1-3, what was the problem that brought dissension in the Church?

____

____

____

What solution was given? (Acts 6:3,4).

____

____

____

____

A good deal of bitterness existed between the Palestinian Hebrews and the Hellenists (Grecian Jews). It must be remembered that this was not a quarrel between Jews and Gentiles—all were Jews. The Grecian Jews were influenced by Greek thinking and customs, resulting in friction between them and the strict Palestinian Jews. Though they had been blessed in many wonderful ways, these apostolic believers were still frail human beings. The Grecian Jews complained that they were being treated as second-class citizens by the Palestinian Jews.

It is a revelation of the grace of God in the Apostolic Church that upon complaint, the church selected six Hellenists (note their Grecian names) and one proselyte to see that the Hellenists were not neglected.

14. What were the qualifications given for the first seven deacons of the Church? (Acts 6:3).

____

____

____

____

The seven men chosen had to be followers of the Lord Jesus Christ—men of character; men who daily, consistently lived the Spirit-filled life; and men of practical ability and tact.

It is interesting to note that the word *deacon* does not appear in the text. But, *diakonos*, the same word used of the ministry of the apostles is used here of these men. These first elected officers were better known as "the seven" (Acts 21:8). They were responsible for the distribution of food and money to the poor, especially to the widows. In that day, widowed women did not have the opportunities for self-support that is possible today and their lives were particularly hard.

The Church faced the problem of dissension in the spirit of Christ. Manifesting strength, not weakness, the Church selected seven men, not Hebrews but Hellenists—men from the very company of those who thought their widows were neglected. And they would minister, not to Hellenists only, but to the Hebrews also. That is the very spirit of Christianity. It overcomes prejudice by heaping upon those who imagine they have been neglected all the honors and responsibilities of office.

<hr>

Discussion
(3 minutes)
Discuss the problem and resolution presented in Acts 6:1-4.
Ask, "What can we learn from the members of the Early Church?"

Discussion
(3 minutes)
Ask group members, "Why was the ministry of 'the seven' so important to the apostles and how is that function accomplished by deacons today?"

✎ **15. Read Acts 6:7. What was the result of correctly handling this potentially disastrous conflict?**

____

____

____

The ever-increasing blessing resting upon the Church may be measured by the fact that a large number of priests became believers. The weight of many testimonies overwhelmed them. The priests, serving as health officers in Israel, examined multitudes of genuine healings which they were obliged to verify. They were convinced of the truth. Their conversion meant the loss of position and exposed them to a double measure of hatred and persecution.

THREATENED BY MARTYRDOM

Until this point, it was the apostles who were singled out for attack. Now the entire Church came under fire. Stephen, one of the seven, became the first martyr. And here we use the word _martyr_ in its accepted sense: one so absolutely committed to truth that he would die rather than violate or deny the truth.

✎ **16. Read Acts 6:8. How was Stephen described by Luke?**

____

____

____

His name indicates that he was a Grecian Jew. And there is a certain prophetic element in his name, for _Stephen_ means "a crown." But his parents could not have foreseen the crown for which he was destined—he was the first Christian to wear a martyr's crown.

✎ **17. Focus on the last words of Stephen in Acts 7:59,60. Of whom does this quote remind you?**

____

____

Stephen was a man full of the Holy Spirit. What fruit of the Spirit do you see him exhibiting at the end of his life?

____

There was a beautiful Christlike quality in Stephen's life. It is seen in the calm, gracious dignity with which he faced the Sanhedrin.

It is believed that Stephen may have belonged to the synagogue of the Libertines (or Freedmen). This was the congregation of former slaves who were most likely set free when Tiberius expelled all Jews from Rome about A.D. 20.

These freedmen, in company with Jews from northern Africa and Asia Minor, challenged Stephen's witness to them concerning the Lord Jesus Christ. When they could not defeat his scriptural testimony, they trumped up false charges against him: treason and blasphemy against God, Moses, and the holy temple.

Stephen was brought to trial before the Sanhedrin because he had said: (1) that God was not the God of the Jews alone, but of the Gentiles also, (2) that His worship was not restricted to the temple in Jerusalem, and (3) that Christ fulfilled the Law's demands, therefore one is not saved by trying to keep the Law. A strange thing happened while

Response
(3 minutes)
Have group members share their responses to study guide items 16 and 17.

Stephen was being accused of blaspheming the law of Moses. The glory that God had given to Moses began to shine on Stephen's face. When asked by the high priest if the charges were true, Stephen delivered a most remarkable message.

18. Read the sermon Stephen preached to the Sanhedrin in Acts 7:1-53. What important figures from Israel's past did Stephen use as illustrations?

____

____

____

____

____

What was the Court's reaction to Stephen's powerful closing? (Acts 7:54-58).

____

____

____

Ask individuals, "Many Christians today have not had to face the threat of death because of their belief in Christ. How would this strengthen the Church if it were a real threat today?"

The theme of his message was the marvelous workings of God's grace and the unbelief of Israel. He showed that God's loving grace cannot be limited to Palestine, Jerusalem, and the temple, as the religious leaders insisted. He proved his point by reminding them that God had been in many different places with several important leaders from Israel's past and blessed them regardless of their location. All of this demonstrated that God was not at all limited to one place. He quoted Isaiah to emphasize this point (Acts 7:48).

Stephen began his message declaring the glory of God (*shekinah*). And this glory shone from his face (Acts 6:15). As he concluded, Luke recorded that Stephen saw the glory of God (Acts 7:55). The final glimpse of Stephen is the deeply moving scene of his martyrdom. His testimony was rejected, and the crowd became a raging mob. On pretense of silencing blasphemy, they rushed on Stephen and cast him out of the city. Without legal right, they stoned Stephen as an act of mob violence. In the Spirit, and with a prayer that was truly like his Lord, Stephen died under a hail of stones.

19. Read Acts 7:58. What young man witnessed Stephen's death?

____

Why was this significant?

____

____

SUMMARY

Any effective Christian enterprise has rarely, if ever, escaped threats that would destroy it. This was no different with the Apostolic Church. The initial church growth was phenomenal. But forces of deceit and dissension from within, and pressures and threats of martyrdom from without, put a strain on those early believers. If nothing else, it made them rely more and more on the Spirit's direction and enabling.

How could the apostles face the wrath of the Sanhedrin? How could Stephen face martyrdom with a prayer for those who stoned him? Because they really believed and accepted the responsibility of the Great Commission.

LET'S REVIEW

1. How did the believers in the Early Church manifest their concern for one another?

____

____

____

2. Where did the idea for Ananias' sin originate?

____

____

____

3. What resulted from the shocking judgment on Ananias and his wife?

____

____

____

4. What was Gamaliel's advice to the Sanhedrin?

____

____

____

5. Describe the first case of dissension recorded concerning the Early Church.

____

____

____

6. What can we do to incorporate into our lives the attitudes demonstrated by Stephen and other early apostles?

____

____

____

____

Review
(4 minutes)

Select two or three items from the "Let's Review" section to review the material in this study.

Closing Prayer
(2 minutes)

Close with a prayer for greater boldness and wisdom in developing a witness and building the Church.

Preparing For Next Session

Remind group members to complete study 4 before the next session.

Group Fellowship
(5 minutes)

Suggest that individuals share the refreshments together after the session.

To witness the triumphs of the Early Church and garner hope for our future.

- Duplicate enough copies of resource 4A, "Whom Should I Tell?" for each group member.
- Four Bible resource books (two Bible handbooks and two Bible encyclopedias).
- Make overhead transparencies of resources 4B, "Qualifications For A Missionary," and 4C, "Effective Evangelism."
- An overhead projector.

FAITH TRIUMPHANT

(All times are estimates. 5 minutes)

Distribute a copy of resource 4A, "Whom Should I Tell?" to each member of the group. Give individuals 3 minutes to read the story. Then ask group members, "What does this story illustrate about each individual's responsibility to witness to the people around him or her and the potential impact one can have on the world as a result?"

Jesus had made it clear that His gospel was intended for the entire world. But this was a difficult fact for the early Christians to grasp. They were strongly bound by the traditions and the prejudices of the past. Going to the Gentile world with the message of Christ was a very real problem to the Early Church.

After the death of Stephen, persecution raged with renewed fury. Saul of Tarsus led the assault. The Church was scattered under the impact of his fierce attacks (Acts 8:1-3). But what initially appeared to be a success for the persecutors turned out to be a triumphant victory for the persecuted.

Persecution spread the gospel to the world outside Jerusalem. Philip went to Samaria. The winning of the Ethiopian eunuch represented a beginning of the fulfillment of the Great Commission. Faith's greatest triumph came in the conquest of Saul, the Church's violent persecutor.

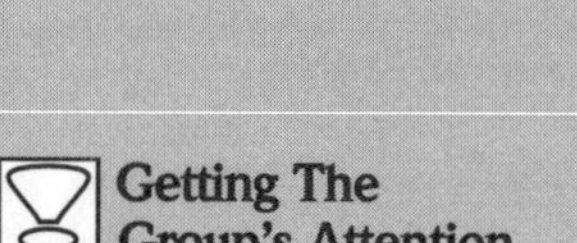

Transition Statement

The Early Church demonstrates that persecution provides opportunity for spiritual triumph.

Victory In Samaria

Driven from the city of Jerusalem, the Christians witnessed for their Lord wherever they went. The devil's plan in scattering the Church was to destroy it. God turned the devil's plan against him and used the scattering of the Church to spearhead a new thrust of evangelism.

1. Philip is the first missionary listed in the Book of Acts, leaving Jerusalem and traveling to Samaria. What was Philip's experience with the evangelization of Samaria? (Acts 8:4-8,12,13).

____

____

____

Philip, one of the seven, went to Samaria. As an evangelist, Philip's message focused on four things: (1) He preached the Word of God; (2) his central message from the Word was Christ, as Messiah and Son of God; (3) he presented "the things concerning the kingdom of God"; and (4) he exalted the name above every name, the name of Jesus Christ.

The preaching of the gospel resulted in a mighty spiritual awakening which was accompanied with unusual manifestations of God's Spirit. Philip witnessed the breaking down of ancient walls that had separated Jews and Samaritans. No doubt, the soil had been prepared for this spiritual harvest.

2. Read John 4:1-42. How did the encounter recorded in this passage prepare the Samaritans for Philip's message?

____

____

3. Look up Acts 8:9-13. How did Simon's reactions to Philip's ministry validate its reality in the hearts of the Samaritan people?

____

____

News of the revival in Samaria reached Jerusalem and Peter and John were sent down to see what was happening.

4. Read Acts 8:14-17. What occurred when Peter and John arrived?

____

____

How do these verses support the truth that the baptism in the Holy Spirit is a separate experience from salvation?

____

____

____

Simon the Sorcerer saw this and was quite impressed. He asked the apostles if they would sell him the ability to "give" the Holy Spirit just by the laying on of his hands.

Response
(3 minutes)

Have individuals share their responses to study guide items 5 and 6.

Read
(2 minutes)

Ask a volunteer to read Acts 8:14-17,20. Reinforce the fact that the baptism in the Holy Spirit is for all believers.

Discussion
(6 minutes)

Have individuals share their responses to study guide item 7.

Ask group members, "Why do you think we don't hear about many experiences with angels in today's society?"

---

5. Given Simon's attraction to signs and wonders (verse 13), how does his request (8:18,19) support the notion that the Samaritan believers spoke in tongues?

____

____

____

6. From Acts 8:20-24, what was Peter's response to that request?

____

____

Simon's attempt to buy spiritual power brought a new word into the vocabulary of the Church—*simony*. (*Simony* means "the buying or selling of a church office or ecclesiastical preferment.") Peter's answer was pungent and clear. And he described Simon's spiritual condition as not having his heart right before God. It was apparent to Peter that Simon was full of bitterness and was still captive to sin. Peter indicated the way of deliverance was to repent and hope that God would forgive.

Simon's answer to the apostle Peter sounded more like the words of a scared sinner than the prayer of contrition. According to ancient tradition, Simon never repented. Later, he turned into a bitter foe of Christianity.

Several gripping truths concerning the person and work of the Holy Spirit are revealed in the account of the Samaritan revival. Those who were converted were encouraged to pray that they might receive the Holy Spirit.

Those who had been led to Christ under Philip's ministry were now led into the baptism in the Holy Spirit under the ministries of Peter and John. It is highly important to note that this spiritual experience is for all the believers (Acts 8:14-17). Just as the 120 had received in Jerusalem, so now the believers in Samaria received. The fullness of the Spirit came to them in answer to prayer as the apostles laid their hands on the seekers.

REACHING TO ETHIOPIA

In fulfillment of Jesus' commission, the first movements in Acts carried the gospel to "Jerusalem, and in all Judea, and in Samaria" (Acts 1:8). Almost invariably, we speak of the door that opened to the Gentiles as the occasion when Peter preached in the house of Cornelius. This may or may not be true. For, without doubt, the Ethiopian treasurer whom Philip met was a Gentile, and his conversion became the opening wedge in the penetration of Ethiopia.

The angel of the Lord prompted Philip to intercept the Ethiopian treasurer on the Gaza Road. It is worthy of special note to study the frequent ministry of angels to the apostles and believers in the Apostolic Church.

7. Look up the following passages and record the instances of angel intervention on behalf of the Early Church: Acts 5:19; 8:26; 10:3,7,22; 12:7-15,23; and 27:23,24.

____

____

____

____

____

____

🖉 **8. Read Acts 8:26-38. What can you learn about effective evangelism from Philip's encounter with the Ethiopian eunuch?**

____

____

____

____

Several important facts about the Ethiopian emerge from the text. First, he was a person of great authority under Candace, queen of the Ethiopians. The name _Candace_ referred to a dynasty, much like the Pharaoh in Egypt, or the Caesar in Rome. The land of Ethiopia under Candace was the kingdom of Meroe, a country of East Africa which lay on the right bank of the Nile from its junction with the Atbara, as far as Khartoum, and then east to the Abyssinian mountains.

The Ethiopian eunuch filled a powerful political position in the government. But political power had not satisfied the deep hunger in his heart. He had turned from the idolatry of his nation and his search had carried him to Jerusalem. There he learned about the true and living God. Now on his way home, he read aloud from the writings of Isaiah. Philip encountered the Ethiopian as he began reading the remarkable prophecies concerning Christ and His suffering.

Philip's question proved to be the key to the Ethiopian's heart. He simply asked if he understood what he was reading. And with the invitation to ride in the chariot, Philip preached Jesus from that magnificent passage in Isaiah 53:7,8 where the death of Christ is compared to the leading of a sheep to the slaughter. Philip recounted the unresisting, sacrificial death of Jesus, the Lamb of God, and explained that His death made possible the forgiveness of the sins of the world.

The Ethiopian asked what is required to qualify one for water baptism and wondered what would hinder him from being baptized. They stopped by some water and both went down into the water and Philip baptized him (Acts 8:39,40).

CONVERSION OF SAUL

The conversion of Saul of Tarsus is undoubtedly one of the greatest events recorded in the Book of Acts, after Pentecost. Following the martyrdom of Stephen, a general persecution broke out against the Christians.

🖉 **9. According to Acts 8:1-3; 9:12, what activities did Saul engage in after the stoning of Stephen?**

____

____

____

The zealous persecutor met the living Christ on the Damascus Road, and he was forever after a new man. His conversion transformed the great enemy of Christianity into one of Christianity's foremost ambassadors. He became the apostle to the Gentiles and the human instrument through which most of the New Testament came to us.

🖉 **10. Read Acts 9:3-19. Describe the events that led to Saul's conversion.**

____

____

____

Overhead
(2 minutes)
Have a group member read Acts 8:26-38.
Display resource 4C, "Effective Evangelism." Help the group see each of these six principles of evangelism modeled by Philip.

Small Groups
(12 minutes)
Divide the group into 2 smaller groups. Distribute one encyclopedia and one handbook to each group. Have one group study the geography and economic condition of Ethiopia at that time. Have the other group investigate the culture and political structure of Ethiopia in biblical times.
Give the groups 5 minutes to gather information. Then allow each group 2 minutes to share what they found.
Ask individuals the following question:
"In what practical ways can you minister to those in your community who reside there on a temporary basis?"

Response
(2 minutes)
Have group members share their responses to study guide item 10.

Because the remainder of the Book of Acts largely records his ministry, it is important to learn the basic facts about Saul's background. Saul of Tarsus is better known to us by the name of Paul. No doubt he assumed this Gentile name to indicate his calling as an apostle to the Gentiles.

Saul was born in Tarsus, a city of Cilicia in Asia Minor. There were two classes of Jews in those days: the Hebraic, or Palestinian Jews, and the Jews of the Dispersion (*diaspora*) who lived in Gentile countries. Saul belonged to the Jews of the Dispersion. Tarsus was a great commercial, political, and educational center. It was one of the three principal university cities of the period, the other two being Athens and Alexandria. Saul was a Roman citizen by birth (it is believed that Saul's father was granted Roman citizenship for service to a distinguished Roman). Among the privileges of a Roman citizen were these: (1) He could not be condemned without a trial; (2) he could not be scourged or crucified; (3) he had the right to appeal to the Roman emperor for justice.

11. Describe how Paul's Roman citizenship benefited the apostle in his later ministry (Acts 16:35-39; 22:22-29).

____

____

Saul studied in the synagogue in Jerusalem under the tutelage of Israel's great teacher, Gamaliel. In addition to studies in Hebrew, the Scriptures, and the laws of Israel, Saul learned the art of tentmaking. His Jewish training gave him the knowledge of the Scriptures; his education in a Gentile college city taught him how to approach the cultured Greek; and his Roman citizenship gave him access to the Roman Empire. Thus, Saul was equipped to carry the gospel to the Roman world.

12. Read 9:19-31 and answer the following questions:

What did Saul do immediately after his conversion? _______________________

____

What was the reaction of those who heard his message? _______________________

____

How did Barnabas bring stability to the situation? _______________________

____

From the Lord's words, it must be concluded that the Holy Spirit had been dealing with Saul before he saw the Damascus vision. Saul surrendered unconditionally. It was a surrender that characterized the rest of his Christian life and missionary labors. Saul entered Damascus in a far different manner than he had expected. He had fallen to the earth a proud, persecuting Pharisee; he arose a humble, brokenhearted Christian.

SUMMARY

Because of the strong faith of the disciples in the Early Church, persecution, when it came, did not serve to extinguish the Spirit's fire, but to fan it. God used men like Philip, Peter, John, and Paul to move out with the Holy Spirit's power and anointing from Jerusalem and extend the good news of Jesus Christ to other people.

It must have been a huge disappointment for the forces of Satan to see their persecution efforts produce just the opposite result from what was intended. And what a crushing blow it must have been when Saul, the most well-known, feared opponent of the Church, switched sides. Jesus took evil and harm and turned it into something for His glory. One of faith's greatest triumphs led the Church forward in expanding its fulfillment of the Great Commission.

<table><tr><td>

LET'S REVIEW

1. Discuss the spread of the gospel to Samaria.

____

____

____

____

____

2. What do you learn concerning the relationship between salvation and baptism in the Holy Spirit as you examine the examples of the Samaritans, the Ethiopian, and the apostle Paul?

____

____

____

____

____

3. Once converted, what message did Saul preach?

____

____

____

____

4. What example for witnessing does the Early Church present for us?

____

____

____

____

____

</td><td>

Review
(4 minutes)

Select two or three items from the "Let's Review" section to review the study.

Closing Prayer
(2 minutes)

Thank God for the persistence and fire of the Early Church and ask for a measure of their faith and courage to witness.

Preparing For Next Session

Remind group members to complete study 5 before the next session. Ask an individual to prepare a report on the time of Caligula, Claudius, and Herod Agrippa. Specific reference to those leaders' influence on the Christian community should be included. Refer the person to a Bible dictionary or encyclopedia.

Group Fellowship
(5 minutes)

Encourage individuals to help themselves to the refreshments supplied and fellowship together.

</td></tr></table>

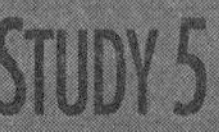

 **Study Objective**

To see how the Early Church overcame prejudices and follow its example in today's Church.

 **What You Will Need**

☐ Ask a group member to prepare a report on the time of Caligula to Claudius and Herod Agrippa and their impact on the Christian and Jewish cultures. Direct the person to a Bible dictionary or encyclopedia for research purposes.

☐ An overhead projector.

☐ Duplicate enough copies of resource 5A, "Dealing With Difficult Situations," for each group member.

☐ Enough blank typing paper for each group member.

Getting The Group's Attention

(All times are estimates. 5 minutes)

Ask group members the following questions:

1. "What traditions or cultural practices prevent you from reaching out to the people different from yourself?"

2. "What can we do to remedy this situation?"

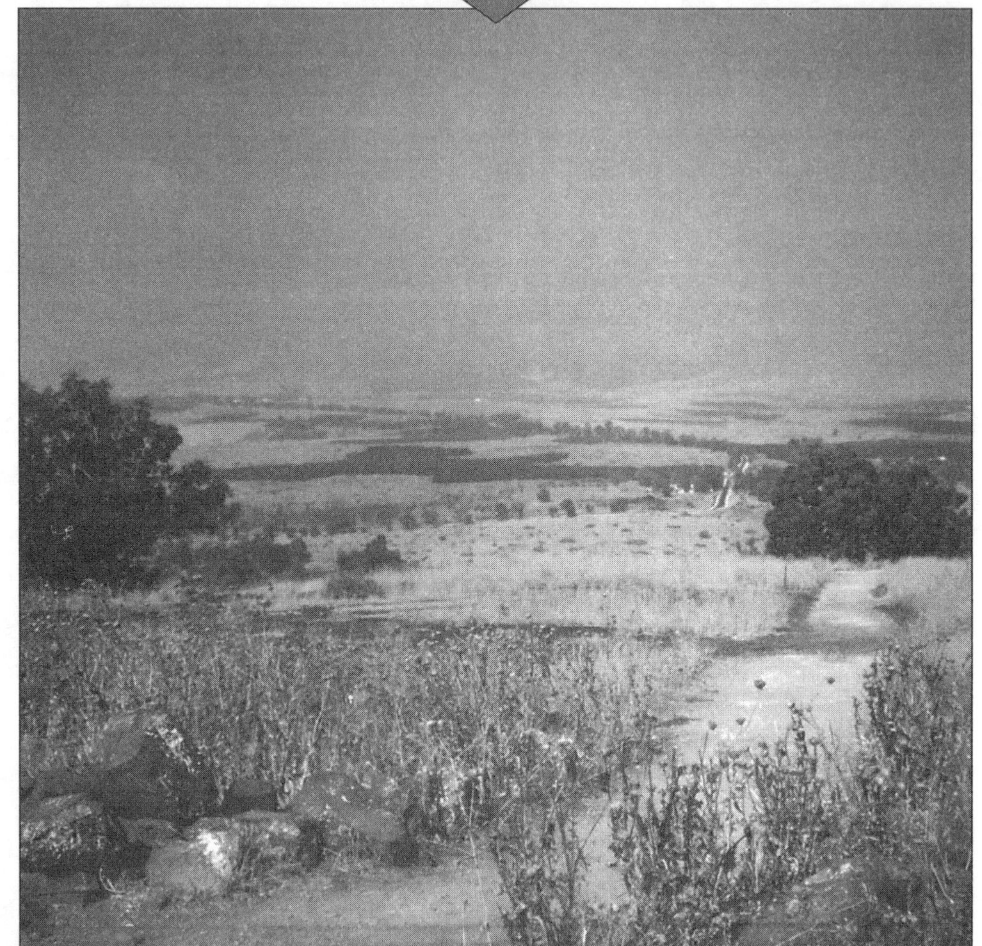

THE SPREADING FLAME

The first Christians were so Jewish in their thinking that it required the power of God to break through their deeply ingrained cultural biases. The most serious of these prejudices was the belief that Jews were in a superior position to the Gentiles. As God demonstrated the truth that the good news was for all people, the Apostolic Church broke loose from the confining, illogical influences of the past.

It seems strange to us that God used the fierce fires of persecution to help spread His flame among the Gentiles. But we must never forget that the first two letters of the word *gospel* spell *go*. And go we must, for His command has not changed. Each of us must be ignited to spread His witness.

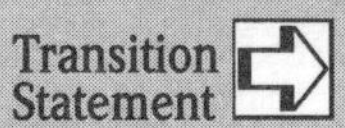 **Transition Statement**

Prejudice can be overcome by viewing others as Jesus sees them.

Revival Fires In Sharon

After the conversion of Saul, the persecution of the believers subsided for a short while. The attention of the Jews was turned toward a new threat against them from Rome. In A.D. 39, Caligula ordered a statue of himself to be erected in the temple at Jerusalem. He commanded that he be worshiped as a god in Jerusalem, as in other parts of the empire. The Jewish leaders were so outraged that they pledged resistance to the death. They organized dissent in front of the Roman governor's palace. An enormous crowd staged a sit-down protest and greeted each appearance of the governor with wild cries. They continued the pressure day after day. Caligula was murdered January, A.D. 41. Claudius became emperor and Herod Agrippa was made king of Judea.

Our last glimpse of Peter was in Samaria, where he ministered with Philip and John to the Samaritans. Now, we follow him outside the city of Jerusalem, as the Holy Spirit moved him to minister in the maritime plains of Sharon. His witnessing carried him to the little villages as well as to the larger cities like Lydda (present-day Lod) and Joppa, the seaport city now known as Jaffa.

Two remarkable miracles were used by the Holy Spirit to help create a great spiritual breakthrough in the maritime area.

 **1. Read Acts 9:32-35. What happened in Lydda to cause people to turn to Christ?**

____

____

Peter came to Lydda and ministered to the saints there. It must be noted that these "saints" were living members of the local congregation. The word *saint* simply means "holy one." There is no scriptural warrant for using this term as a special title for the dead or as a special honor that sets one believer apart from others in the Body of Christ.

Among these saints was Aeneas. For 8 years, as Luke the physician notes, Aeneas suffered from a disabling disease. Luke says Peter "found" Aeneas. Just as Jesus seemed inexorably drawn to the sick and the suffering, so Peter was touched and drawn to the suffering Aeneas. The simplicity of the miracle is striking. No mention is made of times of prayer, Bible teaching, and fellowship which undoubtedly preceded prayer for the sick. Peter's procedure in ministering to the sick is quite uncomplicated and direct; he simply said that Jesus Christ healed them. The compassion of Christ, through Peter, ministered to Aeneas' total being and brought wholeness.

Peter's word of command to rise and make, or take care, of his bed is reminiscent of the ministry of Christ to the sick man lowered through the roof. Peter was there, and no doubt his quickened memory reminded him of both the occasion and the Master's words. Aeneas responded with joy. For 8 long years others had performed menial tasks for him. Now, by the healing power of Jesus Christ, he cared for himself. His healing was instantaneous. The effect of the miracle was widespread. An entire community was engulfed in revival fires.

From here, Peter journeyed on to Joppa at the urgent request of the saints there. Joppa was, and remains to this day, one of Israel's few seaports. Its history is long and is studded with famous names. The building materials for Solomon's Temple were brought to this port. Jonah fled to this place in his attempted escape from God's call. History's greats have come here: Judas Maccabeus, Antiochus, Herod, Vespasian, Omar, Saladin, Richard, Napoleon, and many more.

2. Read Acts 9:36-43. What is interesting about Dorcas' (or Tabitha's) condition at the time Peter was called to come to Joppa?

____

What does the Church's reaction to Dorcas' crisis indicate about the Church's confidence in the ministry of the apostles?

____

Have the individual who prepared the report on Caligula, Claudius, and Herod Agrippa make his or her presentation. Allow for discussion when the presentation is completed.

Have individuals share their responses to study guide item 2.

Ask group members, "What does this confidence indicate about the spiritual condition of the Church?"

3. Compare and contrast the account in Acts 9:36-43 with the one of Jesus and Lazarus (John 11:1-7,11-14,17-45).

____

____

____

____

____

4. Read Luke 8:40-56 to familiarize yourself with the story of Jairus' daughter. What are the similarities between the story of Jarius' daughter and Dorcas' story?

____

____

____

____

There are some beautiful parallels in the raising of Jairus' daughter and Dorcas. And there was no question about how life was restored to these two people. In the case of Dorcas, the news spread throughout Joppa and many came to believe in the Lord because of it.

5. How does the story of Dorcas confirm Jesus' statement recorded in John 14:12?

____

____

THE LEAPING FLAMES

It is entirely possible that Cornelius, as a sincere Gentile seeker, had earnestly examined the religion of Israel. He may have been a "proselyte of the Gate," the term used for Gentile converts to Judaism. He was deeply concerned and most prayerful in his search for the true and living God.

6. Read Acts 10:1,2. What personal information do you learn about Cornelius?

____

____

____

7. Read Acts 10:3-8. What did the angel instruct Cornelius and on what basis?

____

____

Note that Cornelius was not preached to at that time. He was told where he could find a preacher.

8. Read Acts 10:9-23. What seems to be the reason Peter was the apostle chosen to initiate evangelism to the Gentiles?

____

____

____

No doubt the Holy Spirit had been speaking to Peter about the responsibility of reaching out to the Gentiles. And now as he prayed he had the amazing vision of a sheet let down from heaven and on the sheet were unclean animals. Peter learned that the sheet symbolized the world; the four corners of the sheet spoke of the worldwide gathering; and the unclean animals represented the vast Gentile world outside Israel. The Holy Spirit conveyed some highly important lessons to Peter.

9. What did Peter learn about the relationship of Gentiles and Jews to the gospel?

Acts 10:17-20 _______________________________________

____

____

Acts 10:28 _______________________________________

____

____

Acts 10:27; 11:2,3,12 _______________________________

____

____

Peter took Jewish Christians with him to Caesarea. Apparently he grasped the great significance of what this mission involved. He wanted an adequate number of witnesses to all that would be said and done. Time proved the wisdom of this move.

Peter's sermon (Acts 10:24-42) is easily outlined: Point 1, he stated that God is no respecter of persons. Point 2, he reminded his listeners that the spiritual movement began in the ministry of John the Baptist. Point 3, John introduced the ministry of Jesus. Point 4, Christ died on the cross and rose in triumph over death. Point 5, Peter enlarged on Christ's ability to save and how to be saved.

10. Read Acts 10:44-46. What happened, even before Peter had finished his sermon, to the family and friends of Cornelius?

____

____

Read Acts 11:1-18. What was the initial reaction of the believers to this "good news"?

____

____

What initial physical evidence occurred which validated this experience?

____

____

Why would this sign be evidence to the believers?

____

____

____

✎ 11. Read Acts 10:47,48. What occurred next?

____

____

____

____

After the news of this got back to Jerusalem, Peter and the brethren who went with him were called upon to answer the charge that they had gone in to fellowship with Gentiles. The same evidence which proved to Simon the Sorcerer that something miraculous had been given was now used to convince the Church leaders concerning the Gentiles. The sovereign move of God was unmistakable. Peter pointed to the Day of Pentecost as the norm for receiving the Spirit.

THE FLAMES SPREAD NORTHWARD

Instead of extinguishing the flame, persecution scattered the burning embers and began scores of new fires. Some of the believers fled northward to Antioch. As they witnessed to the people there, a gracious revival burst into flame. Antioch was a very important city. It was regarded as the third metropolis of the Roman world. The moral standard of the city was notoriously low. Its religion was a mixture of vile idolatry and degrading superstition. It was a city greatly in need of the message of Christ.

✎ 12. How did the believers in Antioch, both Jew and Gentile, come to know about Jesus? (Acts 11:19-21).

____

____

____

The leaders in this revival move were neither the apostles nor the deacons from Jerusalem. The reason for their success was that the hand of the Lord was with them.

It was not easy for the orthodox Jews in Jerusalem, even though they were Christian, to accept the fact that God was visiting the Gentiles. Barnabas was sent to investigate and to evaluate the situation.

✎ 13. Drawing from passages discussed in previous studies as well as Acts 11:22-24, write a composite description of Barnabas.

____

____

____

____

⇄ **Discussion**
(4 minutes)
Have group members offer examples of modern-day experiences they have questioned but later supported because of God's power working in them.

Ask, "According to Acts 17:11, how are we to test what we see and hear?"

⇄ **Discussion**
(8 minutes)
Distribute a piece of blank paper to each member. Based on the description written in study guide item 13, draw a picture of Barnabas emphasizing his positive qualities in an exaggerated fashion. After individuals are finished, have them display the characters and discuss their insights on Barnabas.

The wrong counsel at this point could have been disastrous. But Barnabas, full of the Holy Spirit, recognized the work of the Lord and was glad. Through the eyes of the Spirit, he saw, not Gentiles, but the grace of God, and he rejoiced. He remained as pastor of this new work.

The result of Barnabas' ministry was that a great number of people were brought to the Lord. People filled with God's goodness and filled with the Holy Spirit still attract the hungry in heart to Christ.

The story thread of the Book of Acts turns now to the life and ministry of the great apostle to the Gentiles—Saul. Saul had retired into seclusion in his childhood home in Tarsus. Barnabas, the good man who could see the grace of God in the Gentiles, was now moved of the Spirit to seek out Saul. He believed that Saul was just the man to help pastor the Gentile church in Antioch. It is significant that Barnabas was the instrument God used on two occasions to save Saul for the work of the Lord. Once, at Jerusalem, when the apostles feared to welcome Saul, Barnabas befriended him. And now, here at Antioch he enlisted Saul in the work of the ministry.

What an interesting situation is presented here. The Gentile church in Antioch was born as a consequence of fierce persecution. Now, the chief instigator of that persecution is selected as one of the pastors of that church.

14. Read Acts 11:26. What term is first used at Antioch?

____

Prior to this time believers were called "followers of the Way," "the brethren," "the disciples," or "the saints." Now, the people of Antioch, whether in derision or sarcasm we do not know, coined this new name.

15. Read Acts 11:27-30. What evidence of Christian unity and love toward the Jewish Christians was demonstrated by the new Gentile Christians in Antioch?

____

____

____

____

THE CHURCH AFLAME

The Church on fire was not free from opposition. A new persecution appeared in the form of a vicious onslaught on the part of King Herod. Herod Agrippa the First was a grandson of Herod the Great, who had attempted to slay the Christ child. Herod Agrippa was caught in a political vise. Holding his authority over the Jews for the sake of Rome, he attempted to please both the Romans and the Jews. Being a keen politician, he saw the political expediency of seeking to destroy Christianity.

16. Read Acts 12:1,2. Who was the first of the twelve apostles to suffer from this new persecution? How was he persecuted?

____

____

Emboldened by the popularity inspired by this pretended zeal for God, the king decided to execute the apostle Peter as well. The Passover Feast delayed Peter's trial. And so Peter spent the days of Passover in prison, closely guarded by 16 Roman soldiers.

(3 minutes)

Ask a volunteer to read Acts 9:18-30.

Ask individuals the following questions:

1. "How would you feel if asked to contribute to the acceptance and discipleship of a new convert if that convert's former lifestyle had been threatening to the Church?"

2. "Why would you feel this way?"

3. "How does Barnabas provide a positive role model?"

(5 minutes)

Have individuals share their responses to study guide item 15. Ask the following question: "What practical ways can you make a person of a different background feel comfortable in your spiritual community?"

(2 minutes)

Have group members share their responses to study guide item 16.

17. What was Peter's experience after his arrest? What was his initial reaction to what was happening to him? (Acts 12:3-11).

____

____

____

The Church was overwhelmed with the suddenness and the ferocity of this new persecution. Prayer was their one mighty resource. They prayed without ceasing. And the praying of a church aflame released the mighty power of God.

Why was one apostle martyred and another released? Questions like these lie in the arena of God's sovereignty. He is God, and we must affirm our full and absolute trust in His love and wisdom. God is too kind to be cruel and too wise to make a mistake.

18. Read Acts 12:12-17. What was the response of those who prayed for this miracle?

____

____

Had they prayed without faith? Not at all. It was merely a human reaction. It was then deemed wise that Peter be concealed until the excitement over his escape subsided.

19. What proof of the reality of Peter's miraculous deliverance is given in Acts 12:18,19?

____

____

The irresistible advance of the spreading flame is shown in contrast.

20. Read Acts 12:19-24. What was the eventual outcome of Herod's attempts to persecute the Church?

____

____

____

SUMMARY

The ability of the Church to survive intense opposition has been a marvel to humankind throughout history. In actuality, the Church has done more than survive in persecution, it has thrived. The secret resource of the Church is the power of the Holy Spirit. So long as He pours in the oil, opposition cannot quench the flame of the Spirit.

What is true for the church as a whole, is also true for its individual members. When we are tried in the fiery test of opposition, God is preparing us to become His cutting edge of truth. The New Testament Church faced an extreme challenge as evangelism spread to the Gentiles. But with the Spirit as their guide, the Church leaders once again demonstrated divine wisdom and love.

1. How did God confirm His Word as Peter preached in Lydda and Joppa?

____

____

____

2. In what way did the Holy Spirit prepare Peter to minister to the Gentiles?

____

____

____

3. How was Peter assured that God received the Gentiles at Caesarea?

____

____

____

____

4. How did the church at Jerusalem react to Peter's report?

____

____

____

5. What caused the message to reach Antioch in Syria?

____

____

____

6. What is the Church's best resource in face of trouble, whether internal or external, social or political?

____

____

____

Review
(4 minutes)

Select two or three items from the "Let's Review" section for study review.

Closing Prayer
(2 minutes)

Close the session with a prayer for Christlike acceptance of all people.

Preparing For Next Session

Remind group members to complete study 6 before the next session. Gather newsletters and written testimonies from missionaries as described in the "What You Will Need" section of study 6.

Group Fellowship
(5 minutes)

Encourage individuals to fellowship together while enjoying the refreshments provided.

Study Objective

To trace Paul and Barnabas' steps as they engaged in the First Missionary Journey and be encouraged to reach out to the unsaved in our world.

What You Will Need

- Newsletters from missionaries supported by your church.
- Duplicate enough copies of resource 6A, "Laborers Together," for each member of the group.
- A world map or globe.
- Written testimonies from missionaries describing how God called them into ministry. (If possible, a visit from a current or retired missionary would be excellent.)
- Create an overhead transparency of resource 6B, "Paul's Journeys." (NOTE: This resource will be reused in later studies.)
- An overhead projector.
- An encyclopedia or book showing modern-day Turkey.
- A Bible encyclopedia.

Getting The Group's Attention

(All times are estimates. 8 minutes)

Distribute a copy of resource 6A, "Laborers Together," to each group member and give them about a minute to read it.

Distribute the missionary newsletters that you brought to the session. Ask volunteers to read the newsletters sharing where the missionaries are and what work they are involved in. As they are being read, point out on the map or globe where each missionary is ministering.

Read the testimonies of the callings of a few missionaries and compare them to the call of Saul and Barnabas.

(If you were able to have a missionary visit the group, allow time for questions following the testimony.)

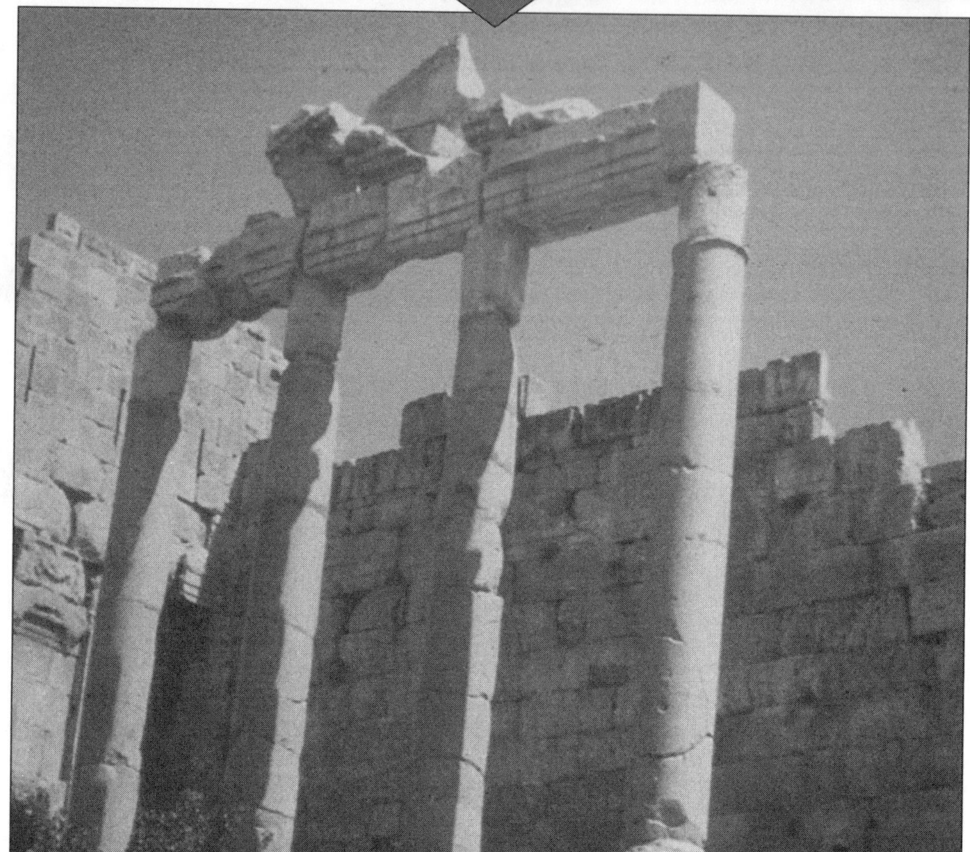

THE FIRST MISSIONARY JOURNEY

The Church began in Jerusalem and gradually penetrated into Judea and Samaria. The door of salvation opened ever wider to the Gentiles and to Israel.

The Book of Acts demonstrates a logical sequence in the development of the spirit of missions. Before there can be a world mission, there must be a church with a world vision; and, before there can be a church with a world vision, there must be men or women responsive to the Holy Spirit's call.

Barnabas and Saul were chosen by the Spirit to be missionaries and they embarked on their first missionary journey. Out of that successful effort emerged the great leadership of the apostle Paul. Missionary work became the passion of his life. Every glimpse of Paul given in the Book of Acts shows him reaching out to those who had never heard the gospel.

Transition Statement

Christians in the Early Church reacted immediately to the impulse of the Holy Spirit to go beyond their homeland to reach the unsaved with the gospel.

46

SENT FORTH

Jerusalem, with the first church and the apostles, seems somehow removed from the mainstream of activity. Antioch in Syria, with its Gentile congregation, has moved into the foreground of missionary work.

Luke mentions five leaders representing five different countries (Acts 13:1). Barnabas is mentioned first, probably because he served as a representative appointed by the Church in Jerusalem. But it must be remembered that he was a Greek-speaking Jew from Cyprus who had been raised among Gentiles. Simeon, called Niger (the Roman name for black), is believed by some to be the Simon of Cyrene who carried the cross for Jesus. Lucius is a Latin name. He came from Cyrene in northern Africa and was reputed to be one of the founders of the church in Antioch (Acts 11:20). Manaen had been brought up with Herod the tetrarch and was believed to be his foster brother. And finally, there was Saul, a Greek-speaking Jew from Tarsus.

These were men of wide knowledge and warm interests. They were not as exclusive or narrow as the Jews in Jerusalem. By education and background, each of these five leaders had touched the Gentile world in different ways. It was in the hearts of these five men that the worldwide missionary program of the Church was born. There was a spiritual concern in their hearts for the salvation of the heathen world.

1. In Acts 13:1-3, what did God instruct the believers in Antioch to do?

____

____

What spiritual climate existed in Antioch when this instruction was given?

____

____

What type of commissioning took place? _______________________

____

____

____

How did the Holy Spirit unfold the great missionary plan? How did He speak? By tongues and interpretation? Possibly, but not necessarily. Prior to this, had not the Holy Spirit spoken directly to Saul, to Ananias, and also to Philip? By prophecy? Again, possibly, but not necessarily. Note that the Holy Spirit referred to a previous call. This suggests that the Holy Spirit had spoken previously to these men on a personal basis, and now He confirmed that which He had said earlier. It is certain that Saul had been called years before this (Acts 9:15).

No matter how this passage is interpreted, Barnabas, Saul, and the church at Antioch sensed that God was in this movement to carry the gospel to the heathen. Perhaps the exact manner in which the Holy Spirit spoke is not specifically revealed so that we would not limit Him to this method.

THE FIRST LEG

Luke records a twofold sending of these first missionaries. They were sent, or released, by the Church; and, of course, sent or commissioned by the Holy Spirit. The Church released two of its valued and needed leaders. They went, undergirded by the love and faith of the congregation. The Holy Spirit guided the Church and the missionaries in this momentous step.

What a modest beginning for world missions! The Church started out on the staggering task of turning a heathen world to God.

Discussion
(3 minutes)

Ask group members the following questions:

1. "Why do you think the Gentile church was the first group to respond to the missions call?"

2. "What might have caused the Jewish church to hold back from missions?"

3. "Which group are you more like, the Gentile church or the Jewish church? Why?"

Testimony
(5 minutes)

Have individuals share their responses to study guide item 1.

Ask a volunteer to share a testimony of a time when God answered a prayer offered up with fasting.

Overhead
(3 minutes)

Place the overhead transparency of resource 6B, "Paul's Journeys," on the overhead projector. Trace the route Paul took based on the material in the parallel column.

Remember that you will use this transparency again. You may not wish to use a permanent marker.

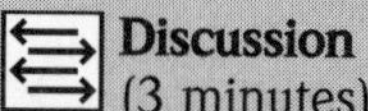

Response
(3 minutes)

Have group members share their responses to study guide item 4.

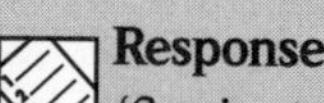

Discussion
(3 minutes)

Ask individuals the following questions:

1. "Why do you think John Mark was necessary?"

2. "How do you suppose his presence impacted the effectiveness of the ministry of the missionaries?"

Response
(2 minutes)

Have an individual share his or her response to both sections of study guide item 5.

2. Read Acts 13:4,5. Who joins Barnabas and Saul on the First Missionary Journey?

____

____

Probably very few of the congregation accompanied the team the 16 miles to Seleucia, the seaport of Antioch at the mouth of the Orontes River. No doubt, these three were scarcely noticed as they boarded the coastal vessel for their journey. Nonetheless, hardly any voyage ever undertaken by humankind has been more momentous in its significance—neither the journey of Christopher Columbus, nor the remarkable space flights in our times. For this Spirit-led move changed the course of human history and has affected humankind for these past 2,000 years.

3. According to Acts 13:4, what island did the team first sail to?

____

____

____

Why this island? Perhaps, because believers of the Antioch church were natives of the copper-rich island. (The Greek word for copper is _cypros_.) Naturally, these believers wanted their families and friends to hear the good news.

They began their work in Salamis on the easternmost end of the island. A pattern for missionary work quickly developed.

4. Read Acts 13:5. What does Paul do upon arriving in Salamis?

____

____

____

Why does Paul choose this venue to begin ministry? Because here the Word of God was reverently treasured. The good news, as the missionaries explained, was the fulfillment of the redemption promised in the sacred Scriptures. The synagogue and the Scripture scrolls supplied three highly important elements to missions: (1) God's house, (2) God's Word, and (3) God's people who believed His Word and worshiped Him, the true and living God.

Here Gentile proselytes to Judaism could also be found. These Gentiles had turned from their false, dead gods and had embraced the worship of the living God of Israel. Later, as we shall see, when the apostles were rejected by the leaders of the local synagogue, they, with believing Jews and Gentiles, left the synagogue and formed the new congregation of those who confessed Jesus as Lord and Messiah.

John Mark is mentioned only in passing as the "helper." He most likely arranged the details of food and lodging for the missionaries.

They traveled the length of the island. It was a journey of about 100 miles. They came to Paphos, the fabled birthplace of Venus (Aphrodite), revered by the heathen as the goddess of love. It was inevitable that opposition would confront them as the light of the gospel challenged the darkness of extreme sexual heathenism.

5. Look up Acts 13:6-11. What form did the new opposition to the gospel take in Paphos?

____

____

____

What did Paul do to deal with it?

____

____

____

Cyprus was governed for Rome by the proconsul Sergius Paulus. The historical and political accuracy of Luke has been repeatedly verified by archaeology. Di Cesnola unearthed a slab with a Greek inscription which contained the name of Sergius Paulus. The proconsul desired to hear the message of truth the missionaries brought, but his attendant tried to turn him from true faith. The attendant's job with the proconsul was quite profitable, and he was not about to give it up without a fight.

The confrontation between Paul and Elymas had all the dramatic elements of Elijah's showdown with the priests of Baal at Mount Carmel. It was all or nothing. Either Christ is Lord of all, or He is not Lord at all!

Paul pronounced a miracle of judgment upon Elymas. There was nothing vindictive about this judicial miracle. No doubt it was Paul's fervent prayer that Elymas might enter into the same spiritual revelation as he himself did during his miraculous meeting with God on the road to Damascus.

✎ **6. According to Acts 13:12, what was the result of this power encounter?**

____

____

____

Miracles are the work of God in which the truth of the gospel is confirmed.

Saul's name is changed to Paul (verse 9). Not necessarily, as some say, out of deference to Sergius Paulus, but more likely as a recognition of his mission to the Gentiles. Saul was his Jewish name and Paul was his Roman name. As he moved more and more among the Romans, he wisely used his Roman name and his Roman citizenship. The name change very likely indicated his complete abandonment to the task of reaching out to the uttermost part of the Roman world.

THE MISSIONARY MESSAGE

When their work in Cyprus ended, Paul and his companions sailed for Perga on the south central coast of Asia Minor. Quite likely their direction was determined in part by the prevailing shipping routes. In Paul's day, Asia Minor was divided into seven Roman provinces of which Pamphylia was one.

✎ **7. In Acts 13:13,14. Luke makes a small reference to John Mark's departure. What atmosphere does Acts 15:37-40 suggest regarding his absence?**

____

____

____

John Mark left the party at Perga and returned to Jerusalem. A number of reasons have been suggested for his departure. (1) As a strict, Jerusalem-bred Jew, he may have looked with alarm at the definite movement toward the Gentiles. (2) He may have been physically weakened by the fevers and illnesses to which the missionaries were exposed. (3) He may have deeply feared the dangers of Paul's planned journey into Asia Minor. It was

Response
(3 minutes)

Have group members share their responses to study guide item 6. Ask individuals the following questions:

1. "How does this event parallel Paul's own experience on the road to Damascus?"

2. "In what way was this action redemptive rather than punitive in nature?"

Small Groups
(6 minutes)

Divide group members into two groups. Give the encyclopedia to one group and ask them to determine the terrain and climate of modern Turkey (ancient Asia Minor).

Give the Bible encyclopedia to the other group and have them find the economic and cultural aspects of Asia Minor at the time Paul and Barnabas traveled to that area.

Give the groups 3 minutes to find the information.

Allow 3 minutes to discuss their findings and what hardships the missionaries may have encountered on this journey.

a path so infested with robbers and so difficult because of mountainous terrain that only the hardiest travelers dared to travel along it. We do not know the exact reason. Whatever John's reason, he left seemingly abruptly.

From the coastal shore at Perga, the missionaries moved northward across the Taurus mountains to Antioch in Pisidia (southern Galatia). Here, the missionaries followed their now well-established practice of going first to the synagogue.

8. Read Paul's sermon preached in Pisidian Antioch in Acts 13:15-42. Compare it with the sermons of Peter (Acts 2:17-39; 3:12-26) and Stephen (Acts 7:2-53). What similarities do you see?

____

____

____

____

Luke has recorded for us the gist of Paul's missionary message in the synagogue at Antioch in Pisidia. It is a singularly appropriate message—well-suited to the Galatians and to us all.

As he began, Paul cited Jewish history. He pointed out God's great redemptive purpose and showed that the promises of God inexorably led to the Lord Jesus Christ. Fulfilled prophecy was emphasized, especially the prophecies related to Jesus' death and resurrection. Paul concluded his message with a strong appeal to faith and the acceptance of forgiveness. He warned against unbelief in light of what their fathers had suffered for their rebellion as recorded in the Old Testament.

Paul's message so profoundly impressed the congregation that many begged to hear it again the following Sabbath. The community's interest was stirred, and the next Sabbath witnessed an amazing crowd present to hear the Word of God.

9. Read Acts 13:44,45. How did the Jews react to Paul's positive reception? Why?

____

____

____

____

It was both a sad and a glad moment for the missionaries. The door to the Gentiles opened ever wider, and the resistance of the unbelieving Jews polarized and stiffened. The missionaries were expelled from the community.

10. As the team of Paul and Barnabas was banished from Antioch, we see a new pattern develop which would be repeated as they went on to Iconium. Read Acts 13:45-52 and record what started to happen at each town.

____

____

____

____

This happened at Iconium, Lystra, and Derbe. Nonetheless, they continued preaching boldly, seeing signs and wonders accompanying their ministry. As they ministered, the listeners were so gripped that many Jews and Gentiles believed.

⇄ Response
(3 minutes)

Have individuals discuss their responses and insights recorded in study guide item 8.

⇄ Discussion
(5 minutes)

Have group members share their responses to study guide item 10. Ask individuals the following questions:

1. "How might have this new pattern positively impacted the ministry of the missionaries?"

2. "In our own lives, how can we be sure when God is closing a door versus just normal opposition to the gospel?"

MINISTRY RESULTS

The first missionary tour was marked with many marvelous manifestations of the power of God. In giving the Great Commission, Jesus promised He would be with His disciples always (Matthew 28:20). Miracles attested to His deity and the truth of His Word. Now the living Lord confirmed the ministry of His disciples with signs and miracles.

It must be remembered that God is omnipotent. Nothing is impossible with Him. But, also remember that God is sovereign. He works in the way He sees best. And He does not always work in the same way.

11. In the recorded reports from Antioch (Acts 13:42-50), Iconium (Acts 14:1-6), and Lystra (Acts 14:8-20), how did the demonstration of God's power in these cities differ?

____

____

____

These differences illustrate that we cannot take what the Holy Spirit does at one time and think this is the way God will always work. This would limit God.

Several things stand out in the healing of the lame man of Lystra. First, he had faith. How had faith been developed in his heart? Paul states in Romans 10:17 that faith is a product of hearing the Word. The lame man heard Paul magnify Jesus as the great physician. Secondly, Paul discerned that faith. And the miracle of discernment was fully as great as the miracle of healing.

12. Read Acts 14:11-13. What mistaken conclusion did the people of Lystra arrive at based on the miracles?

____

____

____

13. Read Acts 14:14-17. How did Paul and Barnabas react to this attention?

____

____

____

14. Read Acts 14:18,19. What resulted from this response?

____

____

____

15. Read Acts 14:20. After this terrible treatment, the team went on. What does this indicate about Paul and Barnabas?

____

____

Response
(3 minutes)
Have individuals share their responses to study guide item 11.

Discussion
(3 minutes)
Have an individual read Acts 14:14-20.
Ask the following question: "What danger exists if one focuses solely on external manifestations of God?"

Paul's recovery was an amazing miracle. The physical punishment must have been terrible. Some believe Paul was beaten into unconsciousness only. Others believe Paul actually died and was raised to life again. In either case, the miracle of God's power was such that he was preserved, or resurrected, and enabled the next day to walk nearly 20 miles to preach in Derbe.

Not all was opposition at Lystra, however. It was there that Paul met Timothy, the young man destined to become his companion and fellow laborer.

MISSION ACCOMPLISHED

The missionaries sensed in the Spirit that their work in central Asia Minor was now completed. As they turned their faces homeward, they retraced their steps so that they might visit each congregation once again.

16. Read Acts 14:21-28. What did Paul and Barnabas do as they revisited each church in Asia Minor?

____

____

____

____

What does this say about the importance of leadership in a congregation?

____

____

____

____

It must have been a moving experience when the missionaries, satisfied that they had done all possible, now commended the people into the Lord's care and departed. There was sorrow in parting, for none could know if or when they would meet again. The First Missionary Journey was now history.

On their return to their home church at Antioch in Syria, Paul and Barnabas related their many adventures for Christ. They had been gone for nearly 2 years and had traveled some 1,400 miles. New congregations had been established wherever they had gone. New and courageous leaders like Timothy and Gaius had been enlisted in the Lord's work. Most important of all the Church had been launched on the vast work of missions.

From here on, the outreach of the Church would be like an ever widening circle, until the entire Roman world would be touched with the good news of Jesus Christ.

SUMMARY

God desires that individual churches (groups of believers) shoulder the responsibility of taking the gospel to the lost through the sending out of those from their midst. Paul and Barnabas, chosen by the Holy Spirit, confirmed by the church leadership, offered themselves for this task.

We see from this first missionary endeavor that difficulties and hardship will be the companions of those who go out in service for our Lord. But, praise be to God, the Holy Spirit will also be there in every situation supporting the ministry of the Lord with signs and wonders. Nothing substantiates the ministry of human beings as the omnipotent power of almighty God working through a dedicated, frail, imperfect vessel.

1. What conditions surrounded the selection and commissioning of the first missionary team?

____

____

____

____

2. What pattern of ministry did Paul and Barnabas adopt as they went from town to town?

____

____

____

____

3. In what ways was Paul's sermon in the synagogue at Antioch in Pisidia an excellent model of missionary preaching?

____

____

____

____

4. What kind of evidences do we see that the Holy Spirit's anointing was on this first missionary team?

____

____

____

____

5. Respond to the following question: "What can I do to advance the missions endeavor of the Church today?"

____

____

____

____

Review
(5 minutes)
Select two or three items from the "Let's Review" section for study review.

Closing Prayer
(2 minutes)
Close in prayer asking God to help individuals to be open to His call to missionary work and be sensitive to the needs of missionaries who are on the field.

Preparing For Next Session
Remind individuals to complete study 7 before the next group session.

Group Fellowship
(5 minutes)
Invite group members to share in the refreshments provided and fellowship together before dismissing.

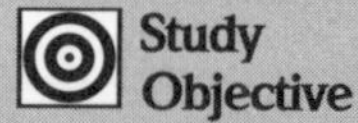

Study Objective

To observe the Early Church's process of conflict resolution and seek to resolve problems in the Church amicably.

What You Will Need

- ☐ Duplicate enough copies of resource 7A, "Which Way Is Right?" for each individual.
- ☐ Prepare an overhead transparency of resource 7B, "Facing The Issue."
- ☐ An overhead projector.

Getting The Group's Attention

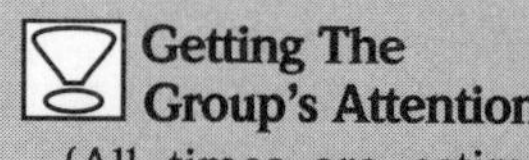

(All times are estimates. 8 minutes)

Distribute a copy of resource 7A, "Which Way Is Right?" to each group member. Give individuals 3 minutes to read and complete the work sheet.

After everyone has written their responses, have group members share their responses to the questions on the work sheet.

THE JERUSALEM COUNCIL

God's free grace comes into direct conflict with religious traditionalism in chapter 15 of the Book of Acts. At stake was the concept that, in Christianity, God accepts people as they are and, through grace, by faith in the completed work of Christ, makes them redeemed, cleansed, forgiven children of God.

The defenders of Jewish traditionalism declared this was blasphemous and unscriptural. It was their contention that Gentile believers must become proselytes to Judaism in order for their faith in Jesus to be a valid, saving faith. They reasoned that if the Gentile converts truly acknowledged Him as Savior, they would obediently embrace and obey the Law as Jesus did.

The resolution of this conflict could determine the face of Christianity forever. As a result, the Jerusalem Council stands as a vital event in Church history.

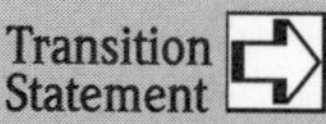

Transition Statement

Conflicts can be resolved when individuals seek to understand one another.

TROUBLE IN ANTIOCH

It is a myth to think that the Apostolic Church was so pure, so powerful, so Spirit-filled that internal strife or dissension did not, and could not, exist. The Church was born and began its ministry in a divided world. It was inevitable that the Church would be composed of people who reflect the divisions and the prejudices of the contemporary scene. The great premise of the gospel is that God is no respecter of persons. His loving grace is extended to the entire world. And the redemption He planned and purchased in Christ is offered with no other limitation than that of repentance and faith. Any person, in any culture, race, or nation is a proper candidate for forgiveness and cleansing through Christ the Lord.

1. Read Acts 15:1-3. What was the new threat to tear the Church apart?

____

____

____

How did Paul and Barnabas react?

____

____

____

What was the solution recommended by the church at Antioch?

____

____

____

The wonder and thrill of the first reports from the missionary journey had scarcely subsided before the most serious threat to challenge the Church appeared at the church in Antioch.

2. Read Galatians 2:4. How did Paul describe the men referred to in Acts 15:1?

____

____

Paul was far more blunt when writing to the Galatian church concerning these individuals than was Luke. In essence, the teaching of these men was that salvation was not completed by an act of faith which received God's grace. They taught that it would be necessary for Gentiles to subscribe to the ceremonial laws of Moses and be circumcised, else all their believing was vain. From their viewpoint, Christianity was a revelation within Judaism, and one could not become a Christian without becoming a proselyte to Jewish traditionalism. Their insistence on circumcision must be understood as an insistence on the observance of the ceremonial law as a means of salvation and communion with God. The requirements of the ceremonial law embraced many other things as well, such as prescribed prayers, kosher foods prepared in a certain way, plus pilgrimages to Jerusalem for certain feast days.

These deeply convinced Jews did not contend for their position superficially or for the mere sake of contention. Their convictions rested on very strong arguments: (1) God had chosen Israel and the physical sign of that covenant was circumcision. Had God's Law been nullified? Had He changed His mind? (2) Jesus himself was a Jew and had submitted to all the Law's demands. Should His followers do less? (3) All the promises of redemption, including the Messiah, had come through Israel. Could they turn away from

Discussion
(3 minutes)
Have individuals share their responses to study guide item 1. Ask group members, "How is internal dissension still apparent in today's Church?"

Overhead
(5 minutes)
Use the overhead transparency of resource 7B, "Facing The Issue," to assist your presentation of the material in the parallel column.

Israel and the promises of God and still claim the redemption those promises offered? (4) Circumcision, in a sense, was like taking up the cross to follow Jesus. It was part of the price that must be paid. Were they unwilling to pay the price?

It was a very positive and convincing position and therefore deeply disturbing. The Church should be forever grateful that when the teachers from Judea came to Antioch they were met face-to-face by Paul and Barnabas.

Paul contended that any attempts to mingle salvation by works with salvation by grace constituted a corruption of the gospel. As he pointed out, if we could save ourselves by our works, then Christ died in vain. His death on the cross was not needed.

Call For A Church Council

Paul and the teachers from Judea faced each other in a discussion that apparently went on for hours. Luke stated there was no small amount of disagreement and dispute.

The elders of the church in Antioch wisely terminated the public debate before the congregation. It was their conviction that a matter of such importance demanded a ruling from the apostles and elders in Jerusalem. They selected Paul, Barnabas, and "certain other of them" to speak for the Gentile believers in Antioch.

It is believed that these others included Luke and Titus. Titus, a Greek, had been converted at Cyprus during the First Missionary Journey.

3. According to Acts 15:3-5, what was the response from the people of Phoenicia and Samaria to the delegation's report of their recent missionary trip?

____

____

____

From the believers in Jerusalem?

____

____

____

The leaders of the challenge were converted Pharisees who were now members of the church in Jerusalem. It comes as a shock to think of former Pharisees as members of the Church. These were the people who had so bitterly opposed Jesus. Of all who listened to them, none understood these ex-Pharisees better than did Paul—he too had been a Pharisee.

It was a serious moment, and the future of Christianity hung in the balance. After all, there were many sects or divisions in Judaism. Would Christianity become just another sect like the Pharisees, the Sadducees, or the Herodians? Would there be a major split over this issue resulting in a church of the Gentiles and a separate Christian group of Jews? Would Christianity, thus divided, be destroyed?

The burden of decision rested with the apostles, elders, and the church in Jerusalem. It is interesting to note that this was not to be a closed-door decision formulated by the apostles.

Luke tells us that much discussion took place, with no consensus arrived at (note verse 7). The position of the traditionalists had been freely and fully expressed. Now, after this long while, the apostle Peter stood to share his experiences. It is remarkable that impetuous Peter could have waited.

4. Read Acts 15:7-11 and summarize Peter's argument.

____

____

Discussion
(4 minutes)

Have group members share their responses to study guide item 3. Ask individuals, "What might be the cause for the differing reactions of the two groups of believers?"

Discussion
(3 minutes)

Ask group members to offer some examples of people who have come to Christ but allow aspects of their previous life situations to affect their beliefs.

Response
(3 minutes)

Have group members share their responses to study guide item 4.

What specific event did Peter refer to in verse 7?

____

____

How did Peter's argument cut through the Pharisees' appeal to tradition?

____

____

____

Peter recounted this event because some of the men present now had severely questioned the propriety of Peter's act of going in with Gentiles and eating with them. As he made his point, the apostle used an unusually descriptive phrase in reference to God. He spoke of Him as the God who searches and knows the heart. And this God who knows and judges in absolute perfect wisdom gave His seal of acceptance to the Gentiles by pouring out of His Holy Spirit upon them. And more, God made no distinction between Jew and Gentile. He gave the same gift to both. One did not have more or less of His redemptive blessing. Most important of all, God purified or cleansed their hearts by faith in Jesus Christ.

Peter then asked the group why they were trying to test God. Did they presume to correct God? Did they think that God made a mistake in saving and baptizing Gentiles in the Spirit? Were they trying to set God straight?

And even more pungently, Peter argued as to why the Jews were trying to put the Gentiles under the Law when even the most orthodox Jew had not been able to uphold its standards.

In one sentence, Peter stated the Christian position with marvelous clarity. He pointed out that all people are offered salvation in the same way, through the grace and mercy of our Lord Jesus Christ. There was divine support that this had indeed happened. What could the others say in response to this?

That ended the discussion. In the profound silence that followed Paul and Barnabas took the occasion to magnify the Lord for the beauty of His saving grace. It could well be that both Luke and Titus gave their testimonies too. Who could deny the evident blessing of God on these two Gentile men! The testimonies of Peter, Paul, Barnabas, and the Gentile brethren so gripped every heart that even the challenging Pharisees were silenced.

THE APOSTOLIC DECISION

The moment of decision had come. James, known as James the Just, the half brother of the Lord, the writer of the epistle that bears his name, and the bishop of the Jerusalem Church, presided over the meeting. It was, therefore, his responsibility to gather together the consensus of the Church, the apostles, and the elders. It must have been a solemn, prayerful moment. Tradition speaks of James as a man who spent so much time in prayer that he had callouses on his knees which some said were as hard as those on a camel. Affectionately, he was called "old camel's knees." As his epistle reveals, his point of view as a Christian was thoroughly Jewish.

5. In a very momentous occasion, James, who was presiding over the meeting, got up and addressed the group with a decision in Acts 15:13-21. What was the decision and what was the rationale?

____

____

____

Discussion
(3 minutes)

Not all tradition is bad. Encourage the group to discuss the following questions and statements:

1. "What are the positive aspects of tradition?"

2. "When does a tradition cross the line and become unhealthy?"

3. "List traditions which have enriched your life."

4. "List traditions that have felt like bondage."

Discussion
(4 minutes)

Have individuals share their responses to study guide item 5. Ask group members, "What does the unanimous agreement of this previously split group indicate?"

In his opening statement James referred back to Peter's remarks. He called Peter by his Hebrew name, Simon. He declared that Peter's words agreed with the writings of the prophets. And then he quoted freely from Amos 9:11,12 and explained that God's ultimate purpose in restoring the glory to Israel will include the Gentile world in that blessing. And in line with that purpose, God is now calling out a people for His name, and He has chosen to include both Jews and Gentiles. With wisdom born of the Holy Spirit, James made a proposal that would impact the growth of the Church throughout the Gentile world. James' suggestion received the support of the whole Church. In the letter, written later, it is stated that all present agreed. It was the kind of unity they all had sensed on the Day of Pentecost. And it lifted their hearts with confidence that they were moving in the stream of the Spirit.

6. Look at Acts 15:19-21 again. What requirements were made of the Gentile Christians to ensure unified fellowship?

____

____

____

Why were the requirements left intact? ______________________________________

____

____

If the Church is to be the common ground of meeting between Jewish and Gentile believers, then it becomes necessary to establish basic rules for that fellowship. Gentile believers are requested to abstain from some activities and foods in which the Jews were not permitted to participate. The areas James, and the others in the Council, listed to be avoided by the Gentiles were things where pagan society vividly contrasted the teachings of the Word of God. Often these practices resulted from or were a part of religious ceremonies. Some were rites connected with the worship of certain gods, such as Aphrodite (Venus), the goddess of love. James wanted the Gentile Christians to remove themselves from this behavior. These customs were greatly offensive to the Jew in the light of sacred Scriptures so in an attempt to build intercultural relationships, Gentile Christians were asked to abstain from them.

7. Read Leviticus 3:17; 7:26; 17:10-14. What do the Scriptures say in reference to the issue of eating blood?

____

____

____

The Jerusalem crisis was ended. It had been a soul-searching ordeal. The decision, once made, brought a new sense of joy and unity. It was agreed that the decision should be delivered to the church in Antioch. This would add weight and dignity to the ruling of the apostles and elders.

8. According to Acts 15:22-32, how did the Church leaders propose to share this decision?

____

____

____

Read
(3 minutes)

Have a volunteer read 1 Corinthians 8:1-13. Following the reading, ask individuals, "How can this passage be reconciled with Acts 15:20?"

Response
(2 minutes)

Have group members share their responses to study guide item 8.

It would be difficult to measure the full importance of the apostolic decision. It clarified the thinking of the churches and tended to unify the convictions of the apostles and the congregations. By putting their thoughts into writing, the letter guarded against any possible omission or neglect of the vital parts of the decision. It tended to prevent misunderstandings that might grow out of the spoken word alone. And it served as a guideline for future questions that might arise to challenge the Church.

We are afforded our first glimpse of Silas in connection with this apostolic letter. He and a brother named Judas, surnamed Barsabbas, were chosen to be the official representatives of the church in Jerusalem to the congregation in Antioch. Something of the stature of these men is revealed in the words—"men that have hazarded their lives for the name of our Lord Jesus Christ" (KJV). These are remarkable credentials, for Judas and Silas lived in an age when every believer faced opposition for his faith and many bore the scars which testified of their loyalty to Christ.

There was a warm spirit of love and kindness conveyed in the apostolic letter. Gentile believers were addressed as brothers and recognized as fellow members in the family of God.

9. The spirit of Acts 15:28 directed evangelism in the first century. How can that same spirit be beneficial in the spread of the gospel locally and around the world?

____

____

____

____

James discerned the importance of emphasizing what had guided the apostolic decision. They had not arrived at this understanding lightly, or solely on the basis of debate, but in the unity of the Spirit. Together they agreed it was important to reflect that assurance in the letter to the Gentile believers.

When the chosen delegation arrived in Antioch, the formal conclusion of the Jerusalem Council was completed. The apostolic letter was read to the assembled congregation and there was great joy throughout the church. The manifested love of the saints in Jerusalem lifted the believers, and they rejoiced for the healing which the letter brought.

SUMMARY

In his play, *The Merchant of Venice*, Shakespeare makes Shylock say, "I will buy with you, sell with you, walk with you, talk with you, and so following; but I will not eat with you, drink with you, nor pray with you."

With remarkable skill, Shakespeare laid his finger on the difference that existed between the Jewish and Gentile worlds. It was a difference that God intended to shatter as He made both to be one in Christ.

There seems to be no belief held tighter or defended more tenaciously than a religious belief. This was the situation between the Pharisaic believers and the influx of Gentile believers from outside of Jerusalem. The very thing (the letter of the law) that the believers of the Pharisees prided themselves in, was threatened to be no longer significant. Fortunately, the proof of the manifestations of the Holy Spirit, along with divine wisdom and guidance given to the Early Church leaders, were powerful enough to show to the Church that God was desiring to do a new thing. They could no more stand in the way of it than the Sanhedrin could stop the advance of Christianity.

God identified himself with humankind in His suffering. His Son came to the lowest depths of humanity's need so that none could feel excluded. This infinite grace is intended for all people. There are no requirements to be met or human standards to live up to. God accepts us as we are and works with us as we grow in our relationship with Him.

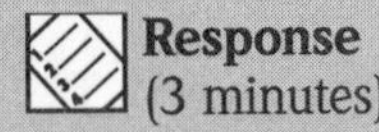

Response
(3 minutes)
Have individuals share their responses to study guide item 9.

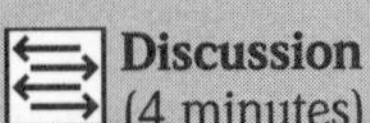

Discussion
(4 minutes)
Ask group members the following questions:
1. "What do the events recorded in Acts 15 teach us about cooperation between the old and the new within a church?"
2. "How can unity of spirit benefit the Church today?"

LET'S REVIEW

✎ 1. What claims did the men from Judea bring to the church in Antioch? Did they have support for their position?

____

____

____

____

✎ 2. Why did Paul insist that Gentile converts not be required to observe the law of Moses?

____

____

____

✎ 3. How was the decision at Jerusalem made? What can we learn from this?

____

____

____

✎ 4. Summarize the decision made in the Jerusalem Council.

____

____

____

✎ 5. Why was the apostolic letter important? Who was selected to deliver it?

____

____

____

____

✎ 6. How can we cultivate a spirit of unity in the Church today?

____

____

____

____

STUDY 8

WESTWARD TO EUROPE

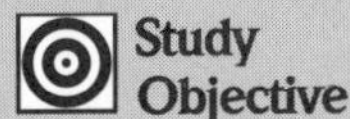

Study Objective

To study Paul's sensitivity to the Holy Spirit during the Second Missionary Journey and determine to listen to the guidance of the Spirit.

What You Will Need

□ The children's book, *The Little Engine That Could*, or another children's book that demonstrates persistence.
□ Locate and reuse resource 6B, "Paul's Journeys."
□ An overhead projector.
□ Ask 2 group members to prepare a 3-minute skit about Paul and Silas' crossing of the Cilician Gates, giving reference to terrain and weather conditions.

Paul and Barnabas had returned to Antioch. Judas and Silas accompanied them from Jerusalem, bearing the official letter which recorded the decision of the Council. Paul carried a copy of it with him on all succeeding missionary ventures. The letter was read to the congregation in Antioch and was received with joy. Judas and Silas also ministered to the Church and exhorted them to continue the missionary outreach they had so valiantly begun.

By this time Paul had given approximately 13 years to Christian service. He had traveled far; he had worked hard; and he had suffered a great deal for the cause of Christ. Perhaps his most difficult burden was the opposition he endured at the hands of his Jewish brethren. Smaller-spirited individuals might have given up. This was not Paul's reaction. As long as he had strength to go on, he was determined to witness for Christ.

Getting The Group's Attention

(All times are estimates. 8 minutes)

Without preliminary explanation, begin reading *The Little Engine That Could* (or another book you brought to the session).

After reading the book, have group members share personal experiences or stories of individuals they know who have persevered against extreme opposition.

Ask individuals the following questions:

1. "What kept the person going?"

2. "How can tough experiences help in your spiritual life?"

Developing sensitivity to the leading of the Holy Spirit will help us to act in God's timing.

Transition Statement

It comes as no surprise that Paul resolved to return to the churches established on the first tour. The first missionary experience created within Paul the driving desire to return and continue this work. And though he and Barnabas ministered with joy in Antioch, there were also many others who shared in the work. His heart was with the Gentile converts in Galatia.

1. Another opportunity to derail the gospel message is recorded in Acts 15:36-40. Summarize the events which transpired.

____

____

What was the positive result of this unfortunate situation?

____

____

When Paul proposed a return missionary trip, Barnabas wanted to take John Mark along. The disagreement between Paul and Barnabas was unfortunate. However, now two missionary teams entered the field, and the work was carried forward.

It seemed regrettable that these two strong men should be parted. They had shared so much together. Perhaps Paul owed more to Barnabas than to any other person. At the time of his conversion, it was Barnabas who offered him friendship even though the apostles in Jerusalem feared and turned from him. It was Barnabas who sought him out in Tarsus and invited him to Antioch as a fellow minister. And now, this greathearted man wanted to give John Mark a second chance and Paul would not consent to it.

The separation is all the more regrettable when it is recognized that both of these men were right. Paul was right when he insisted that missionary work demanded courage and steadfast endurance. But then, Barnabas was also right when he insisted that John Mark needed loving encouragement. He was right when he insisted that the element of compassionate understanding should never be absent in our dealings with one another.

Barnabas, the man of goodness, discerned the grace of God in the Gentiles at Antioch. He recognized the potential greatness of a person like Paul. And Barnabas perceived great possibilities in young John Mark and was determined that he be given another chance.

Tradition says that Barnabas founded many churches in Cyprus and died there as a martyr. John Mark went on to be a fellow laborer with the apostle Peter. He wrote the second book of the New Testament, which bears his name, and in due time was reunited with Paul.

2. Read the following passages to determine the members of Paul's ministry team.

Acts 15:40 ____

Acts 16:1-3 ____

3. What do the following passages communicate concerning Paul's confidence in Silas? (Acts 15:22,32,40; 2 Corinthians 1:19; 1 Thessalonians 1:1; 2 Thessalonians 1:1).

____

____

Silas joined the missionary team and brought with him some very impressive credentials. He traveled with Paul to Europe, sharing ministry responsibilities and persecution as they went.

This second missionary trip is directed by the Holy Spirit into Europe, giving the Church a broad new dimension and altering the course of world history. They ventured northward by land over Syria and then into Cilicia. This is the first mention of churches in these parts. Cilicia was Paul's own native country. It lay northwest of Antioch and was in Asia Minor proper.

The land route to Derbe was a distance of some 120 miles. Going westward across the Taurus mountain range, the missionaries probably traversed the famous gorge, 80 miles long, known as the Cilician Gates. Every great military force passed this way, from Cyrus, Alexander, and the Romans, to the Saracens, and the Crusaders. It was a fearsome gorge.

Coming into Galatia from the east, Paul returned first of all to Derbe, then to Lystra and Iconium.

✎ **4. Read Acts 16:1-5. This is now the third time that Paul has visited the churches in these towns. How is his reception different from the first time he visited them? (Acts 14:1-20).**

____

____

The maturity of the churches was evident. As though pleasantly surprised, Luke recorded the discovery of young Timothy. His mother, grandmother, and possibly Timothy himself, had been converted under the ministry of Paul. In the intervening years Timothy had developed into an outstanding young disciple.

✎ **5. Refer to 1 Timothy 4:14 and 2 Timothy 1:6. What set Timothy apart as ministry material?**

____

____

Timothy had the confidence of the elders, and when it was learned that Paul would like a young man to join the team, the brethren warmly commended Timothy to Paul. The brethren and Paul laid hands on Timothy and set him apart for the Lord's work. As they prayed, God gifted this young man for the work of the ministry.

✎ **6. Read Acts 15:1,2 and 16:3. How do you reconcile these two passages concerning the need to be circumcised?**

____

____

Because Timothy was the child of a Jewish mother he was considered a Jew. Due to that Paul expected a different demonstration of faith from Timothy than he did from other new believers. In the case of Titus, the young Greek, Paul refused to permit the same act (Galatians 2:3).

✎ **7. Look up the following passages and record how these verses indicate the coming and going of Luke with the missionary team: Acts 16:10-17; 20:5-15; 21:1-18; and 27:1 through 28:16.**

____

____

The Greek physician, Luke, joined the missionary party and coupled the healing arts with a gentle spiritual ministry. His most notable contribution consisted in the writing of two books of the New Testament—the Gospel of Luke and the Book of Acts. Luke's presence with the missionary team is modestly recorded by what are called the *we passages*. The missionary team now consisted of four members: Paul, Silas, Timothy, and Luke.

Overhead
(2 minutes)

Use overhead transparency of resource 6B, "Paul's Journeys," and trace the path of the second journey through the material provided in the parallel column. (NOTE: This resource will be used one more time.)

Presentation
(6 minutes)

Have the individuals who prepared the skit give their presentation. After the skit, allow the other group members 3 minutes for questions and discussion.

Discussion
(3 minutes)

Ask group members the following questions:

1. "Besides going as a helper, what is the long-term benefit of Timothy joining the team?"

2. "How can this principle of training up young leaders be continued today?"

Response
(3 minutes)

Have individuals share their responses to study guide item 7.

8. Read Acts 16:4,5. What did this team do as they went westward and what were the results?

____

____

ON TO EUROPE

Paul's next target was Asia. The Asia referred to here is a limited area of Asia Minor, later made familiar as the locale of the seven churches of Revelation (Revelation 1:20).

9. Read Acts 16:6-8. Up to now there has been much evidence of the Holy Spirit's work in the ministry of the missionary team through signs and wonders. Now we see Him working in another manner. What was it?

____

____

____

10. What do the events recorded in Acts 16:6-8 reveal about the process of being led by the Holy Spirit?

____

____

____

The capital city of this region was Ephesus. Later, Paul evangelized this city and thousands were led to Christ. But at this moment the Holy Spirit did not permit him to enter. And so Paul turned northward to Bithynia, the region bordering the Black Sea.

One door after another closed before him, but in this blessed hindering by the Holy Spirit Paul was being directed toward the greatest open door of his ministry. He had to learn, as must we all, that the Spirit directs in different ways. But it is certain that when God closes one door, He opens another.

Paul came to Troas, the most important seaport on the eastern shore of the northern Agean Sea. A few miles removed from Troas was the site of ancient Troy. This did not interest Paul but the cities of Europe drew him like a magnet. Across the narrow stretch of water lay Greece and Rome. It was a setting well calculated to fire Paul's holy ambitions.

11. Read Acts 16:9. Describe the vision given to Paul.

____

____

12. Once they recognized the Spirit's leading, what was the team's response? (Acts 16:10).

____

____

Paul and his group had to sail first to the rocky island of Samothrace, and from there to Neapolis. From Neapolis it was a short distance to Philippi, the chief city of that part of Macedonia.

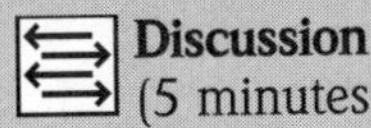 **13.** One has to think that Paul and his company had some sort of idea or plan for this trip when they left from Antioch. What does the switching of directions in their ministry say about the missionary team?

____

____

Why was Paul attracted to the large cities? He saw the opportunity that concentrations of population afforded, but more, he saw them as centers for evangelism. The city, to Paul, was as the hub of a wheel, and the spokes represented the lines of evangelism that flowed out of the center in all directions.

But Philippi was more than a chief city; it was also a Roman colony. This meant that its citizens were counted as citizens of Rome, with the political rights and privileges of Roman citizenship. To plant the Church of Jesus here was the opening wedge in the entrance to the Roman Empire—and this was Paul's true goal: to establish churches throughout the Imperial Empire.

 **14.** Read Acts 16:13-15. How did God provide the missionary team a toehold in the city of Philippi?

____

____

The beginning of the work in Macedonia was very humble. Apparently there was no synagogue in Philippi, so Paul looked for prayer groups. He found a small gathering of women outside the city near a riverbank. And as someone has whimsically remarked, "The man of Macedonia turned out to be a woman—Lydia, the seller of purple." Lydia became Paul's first convert in Europe. She must have been a wealthy woman to deal in such valuable merchandise. Purple dye was used in the most expensive cloth of the day. After she had been converted and baptized in water, she urged the missionaries to be guests in her home.

15. As in several other locations, the missionary team encountered disruptive forces in their evangelism efforts. Read Acts 16:16-24. What was the nature of the disturbance at Philippi and what was the result?

____

____

The slave girl's masters made great gain out of what they claimed was her supernatural ability to tell fortunes, to predict the future, or to give advice on what were the best days for business, for weddings, etc. She was said to have a spirit of divination, or literally, _a spirit, a Python_. Python, from the Greek verb _to rot_, was the great serpent which Apollo killed on Mount Parnassus and left to rot. Hence, Apollo was called _the Pythian_, and fortune-tellers who were supposed to be inspired by Apollo, with wild cries and convulsive movements, were said to have a Python.

But when this girl caught a glimpse of Paul and his companions, she followed them crying that they were the servants of the most high God and were showing the way of salvation. Paul endured this for many days and then, grieved (worn out), he rebuked the spirit and commanded him to come out in the name of Jesus Christ. The girl was instantly delivered.

The owners had no spiritual perception, but they knew that whatever had given this girl unusual powers was gone, and with it their hope of further gains. In their rage they dragged Paul and Silas before the Roman magistrates. They charged that, as Jews, the apostles taught customs not lawful to Romans. Anything anti-Roman was considered a serious offense. There was no semblance of a trial. The clothing of the missionaries was stripped from them, they were fearfully beaten with the rods, and thrown into an inner dungeon. They lay in a dark, unventilated room, their feet fixed in torturous stocks, and their backs bruised and bleeding.

16. Read Acts 16:25,26. How did Paul and Silas respond to their treatment?

____

____

____

How did God respond to their predicament?

____

____

Injustice and beatings could not stop the flow of the inner stream of the Spirit. God honored their praise and worship. There was no rational explanation for what Luke described—except God.

17. What was the jailer's reaction from verse 27?

____

____

What was the end result for the jailer? (Acts 16:28-34).

____

____

We can understand the jailer's reaction. He sensed the supernatural, yet he was well aware of his legal responsibility for each prisoner. Under Roman law if prisoners escaped it was his life for theirs. His next actions continued with the same dramatic suddenness as the earthquake. The jailer's question is the most important question a person can ask. The directness and simplicity of Paul's answer are noteworthy.

18. What demand did Paul make of the magistrate according to Acts 16:35-40?

____

____

Paul was not unwilling to suffer for the gospel's sake, but he wanted the civil authorities to realize that in persecuting individuals for their Christian faith, they had violated both the laws of humanity and of God. Paul refused to allow the magistrates to quietly close the matter of the brutal public flogging and unjust imprisonment meted out to Silas and him. As Roman citizens their rights had been violated. They insisted that the magistrates publicly acknowledge their error and come to the jail in person in order to close the case. In so doing, Paul and Silas were publicly vindicated, and the new fellowship of believers in Philippi was placed in a more favorable position in the community.

SUMMARY

Paul was stirred to bring the message to the heathen world which had not as yet heard. After the decision from the Council in Jerusalem, he was ready to go back out in missions work. Personal conflicts could not stop these early missionaries. When Paul received the Macedonian call, he was moved to the depths of his soul. This led to the historic march of Christianity onto the shores of Europe. Despite his circumstances, Paul continued in his work for the Lord.

LET'S REVIEW

1. Who accompanied Paul on his Second Missionary Journey? Why not Barnabas?

____

____

____

____

2. What biblical evidence demonstrates that Luke joined the missionary party at Troas?

____

____

____

____

____

3. It is apparent that Paul focused his ministry efforts in the large cities of his day. Why? What lessons can we learn from this practice today?

____

____

____

____

4. What was the outcome of the persecution received at Philippi by Paul and Silas?

____

____

____

____

5. How can a person balance exercising his rights with the idea of laying down one's life for Jesus?

____

____

____

____

Review
(5 minutes)
Select two or three items from the "Let's Review" section to review study.

Closing Prayer
(2 minutes)
Close with a prayer for a new openness to the guidance of the Holy Spirit.

Preparing For Next Session
Remind group members to complete study 9 before the next session.
Ask one of the group members to make a cultural, historical, and geographical report on Athens, A.D. 49-52.

Group Fellowship
(5 minutes)
Invite individuals to share in the refreshments provided before leaving.

THE ONE TRUE AND LIVING GOD

The initial impact of the gospel on Europe was tremendous! Paul and Silas had a difficult struggle in the city of Philippi, but they won a great victory.

The assault on the pagan world had begun in earnest. At Thessalonica and Berea, the missionaries were aided by the synagogue and the written Scriptures in their efforts to present the true and living God. In Athens, they came into direct confrontation with the learned people and the pagan philosophies of ancient Greece. Behind the glory and beauty of the literature and the art of Athens were the degrading idolatry and superstitions that filled the city.

An issue consistently faced by Paul and his team was polytheism or the belief in multiple gods. Paul's message was uncompromised—there is only one true and living God.

Understanding one's audience will aid in the effective spread of the gospel.

THE GOD OF THE SCRIPTURES

Thessalonica was about 100 miles southwest of Philippi. It was the largest city in Macedonia and noted as a commercial center. Highly important to Paul was the synagogue of the Jews which he found in the city. The synagogue, with its scrolls of the sacred Scriptures, provided Paul the best opportunity to proclaim the true, living God. Luke gives an insight into the Pauline method of ministering.

1. Read Matthew 12:9-12 and then Acts 17:1-3. Paul followed Jesus' example of going to the synagogue. On what did Paul base his arguments?

____

____

What was the point he consistently tried to prove?

____

____

According to Acts 17:2, Paul "reasoned with them." The Greek word for *reasoning* is almost letter for letter the same as our word *dialogue*. The common ground of agreement between Paul and the men in the synagogue was their mutual faith in the Scriptures as the Word of God. The dialogue that ensued was a good deal like the question and answer period in a classroom.

Paul helped them to see the deeper meaning of the Word and the relationships of the great redemptive truths. No doubt the Book of Romans provides an excellent example of Paul's method of Bible teaching. He laid the types and the prophecies concerning the Messiah alongside the life of Jesus and then gave his reasons for believing that Jesus is the Messiah.

2. According to Acts 17:4, what was the result of the dialogue?

____

____

3. Read Acts 17:5-9. How did the Jews react to the spiritual revival?

____

____

How is this reminiscent of the Jews' treatment of Jesus?

____

____

Before the magistrates, the accusers made two charges against the missionaries. These men have turned the world upside down and are going to do the same thing here. In a way, this was a flattering charge. It testified to the power and the wide influence of Christianity. It was more of a compliment than a complaint.

They also charged Paul and Silas with working against the laws of Caesar. This was serious because it charged the missionaries with treason. The complaint was skillfully planned, and it cleverly distorted the teachings about Christ and His kingdom. It was not difficult for them to make it appear that the teachings of Jesus constituted a threat to the authority of Caesar in his own empire.

The authorities were in a dangerous position. Treason was a sensitive point with the Romans. No overt treasonable act had been committed so the authorities decided to place

Jason under a sort of peace bond. He was required to post a large deposit of money which would be forfeited if anything illegal or treasonable were done by him or the missionaries. This meant that Paul could not return to Thessalonica without endangering his friend Jason.

4. According to Acts 17:10, how did Paul respond to this dilemma?

____

____

____

5. Read 1 Thessalonians 2:17-20. How did Paul feel about leaving the Thessalonians in the manner he did?

____

____

In Berea the pattern of events followed almost the same sequence as in Thessalonica. Paul ministered in the synagogue and there was a strong spiritual response. Many of the Jews and also many of the outstanding Greek men and women of the community believed.

6. Read Acts 17:11,12. What did Luke praise the Berean Christians for doing?

____

____

____

7. Read Acts 17:13,14. How does this continual attack of Satan prove the effectiveness of the gospel message?

____

____

____

The Bereans' minds were open to the truth of God's Word. They were willing to listen. What they heard had to check with the Scriptures or they were not willing to accept it. For them, the Word of God was the final authority.

Silas and Timothy stayed in Berea while Paul went on to Athens. From Athens Paul sent word for his companions to join him as soon as possible.

A CITY FULL OF GODS

In Paul's day, Athens was one of the three most celebrated cities in the ancient world. Jerusalem was considered to be the center of true religion. Rome was famous as the political capital of the world. And Athens was considered the literary and art center of the world. It was a city rich in culture and abounding with schools of philosophy.

Pliny, a historian, declared that at one time Athens boasted over 3,000 public statues, with thousands more in private gardens and homes. On every gateway and porch could be seen the protecting god of that home or place of business. In one street there stood before every house a square pillar carrying upon it a bust of the god Hermes. A Roman satirist once sarcastically remarked that it was easier in Athens to find gods than to find people.

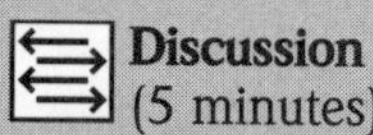

Discussion
(5 minutes)

Have individuals share their responses to study guide item 6. Ask group members the following questions:

1. "What two spiritual characteristics are demonstrated by the Bereans in Acts 17:11?"

2. "How far did the Jews have to travel to stir up trouble?"

3. "What would spur them to such a drastic action?"

Presentation
(8 minutes)

Have the individual who prepared the report on Athens give the presentation.

Allow 3 minutes following the presentation for questions from the other group members.

✎ **8. Based on this description of Athens, do you think evangelism would be easier or more difficult here? Give an explanation for your response.**

____

____

____

____

One of the greatest universities of the Roman Empire was in Athens. The streets of the city buzzed with the conversations of students. The names of the great Athenian philosophers, writers, and artists such as Socrates, Plato, Aristotle, Phidias, and Pericles, are revered to this day.

But underlying all the artistic beauty and splendor of Athens was the demoralizing influence of idolatry. The Athenians worshiped gods who were shameless and open in their loves and hates. Fornication, adultery, and rape were not considered crimes or sins. The gods gave license and sanction to every passion and lust. Devotees of Aphrodite, the love goddess, committed fornication in the temple as part of their ritual of religion. Followers of Bacchus lifted libations to their god in drunken, bacchanalian feasts.

✎ **9. According to Acts 17:16,17, what was Paul's response to this moral and religious cesspool?**

____

____

It was the paradoxical sight of beauty in literature and art and the degeneracy of character and morals that gripped and stirred Paul's heart. His soul burned with indignation that all this beauty, wealth, learning, and genius could be dedicated to idols instead of to the true and living God. What a contradiction that in a city where philosophers boasted of the freedom of mind and thought, four out of five persons were slaves.

✎ **10. How does Paul's action provide guidance to contemporary Christians who face similar situations?**

____

____

He appealed to the devout persons but received no response. The agora was the marketplace, the great central square of the city. In the manner of Socrates, he stopped people to talk with them, to challenge them. It was in this way that he met a new audience.

✎ **11. According to Acts 17:18-21, who agreed to listen to Paul? Why?**

____

____

The Epicureans were the materialists, the atheists, the hedonists of their times. They taught that pleasure or happiness was the true goal and meaning of life. They fully subscribed to the idea, "Eat, drink, and be merry for tomorrow we die." The Stoics were in essence the same as modern pantheists. To them, God was everything, everything was God—including themselves. They were fatalists and considered absolute apathy the high-

---

est moral attainment. They taught that life was governed by fate and there was no individual life after death. It was a hopeless, comfortless philosophy.

These thinkers listened to Paul and argued with him. They called him a "babbler," literally, a "seed picker." They contemptuously charged him with picking up ideas here and there and trying to pass them off as his own original thinking. Others charged that he was teaching some foreign religion about one Jesus and "Anastasia." The Greek word for resurrection is *anastasis*, and in their ignorance they thought Paul was talking about two Gods—Jesus and one called Anastasis.

There were strict laws that governed the preaching of any new or foreign religion; therefore, Paul was brought before the Areopagus. The Romans had granted the Athenians a measure of self-government under the court Council of Areopagus. It was their responsibility to decide what gods and what teachings were permissible, or good, for Athenians.

It is not clear whether Paul was ordered or invited to appear before the court of Areopagus to explain his belief. They had the right to permit or to forbid Paul to preach his message in Athens. Paul's famous Mars' Hill address was delivered to the Council.

12. Read Acts 17:22-31. How is Paul's approach different with this audience than if he were speaking to Jews?

____

____

____

Paul was quite diplomatic when he spoke. He began in the style of Demosthenes, the famous Athenian orator, "Men of Athens." It is quite certain he did not say, "You are too superstitious," but rather, "You are very religious." In his desire to win these people it is not likely that Paul would begin by denouncing them. In their religious zeal they had erected an altar to the unknown God. Paul declared that he had come to talk with them about the God they instinctively longed for and worshiped, but did not know.

Paul revealed the unknown God. How clearly Paul preached the doctrine of God. God is the Creator. In one stroke, Paul dismissed all the gods created by human minds and hands. The true and living God created the heavens, the earth, and all life. God is infinite. God cannot be contained in anything human beings have created. He is greater than His creation, and He cannot be confined to a temple as idols are housed in shrines by people. Nor is God "worshiped" or cared for by individuals' hands. The thousands of idols had to be clothed with silver, gold, and costly garments and carried to banquets and state functions. The true God gives life and breath to all, and He asks for our love and trust in return. God is the sustainer of all. There is a basic unity in humankind. In Acts 17:26, Paul states that God made all nations from one individual. This is a true, scientific fact which the microscope and the test tube reveal. There is no constituent difference in the blood of human beings, regardless of race. Thus, in God's sight, there are no superiors nor inferiors. In this statement, Paul struck a hard blow at the Athenian view that any less cultured than they were barbarians.

13. What does the apostle Paul's ability to interact with men and women of different levels of culture, education, and background encourage us to do to reach the vast people groups of our world?

____

____

____

____

Paul quoted the Greek poets who declared that humans are the "offspring" of God. Because human beings are made in the likeness of God, we should not think of God as being made of gold, silver, or sculptured from stone by skillful hands. Idolatry degrades humankind because it degrades God. God is the judge of all. God "winked at" or tolerated the sins of people's ignorance because He deals with humankind in His patience and

---

Discussion
(3 minutes)

Have group members share their responses to study guide item 12. Ask, "How does Paul's tactic in Athens fit his statement in 1 Corinthians 9:22,23?"

Response
(4 minutes)

Have individuals share their responses to study guide item 13.

mercy. Paul continued, stating God does not approve of the polytheism (the worship of many gods) of the pagan; God in His kindness has merely tolerated these sins of ignorance until the time when He would more fully reveal himself in and through Jesus Christ. This He has now done. Hence, God commands people everywhere to repent, to put away idols, and worship the one true and living God.

At the climax of his message, Paul spoke of the righteousness of God which demands that He judge all people. God is righteous, and He requires that humans be righteous too. In addition to being righteous, God is also redemptive. God gave His Son, the Lord Jesus Christ, to die for our sins and to rise again that we might be brought into right relationship with God. This is the good news that God, the Righteous One, has provided a way whereby a sinful human may be cleansed, forgiven, and have the hope of everlasting life with God.

 **14. Refer to Acts 17:32-34 for the outcome of Paul's message on Mars' Hill. What were the three reactions to the message?**

____

____

____

____

The materialism and the pantheism of the Epicureans and Stoics left no place for the concept of God as Paul preached it. If Paul were right, then they should repent. But it was laughable to think that Paul could be right! There is no transcendental God; there is no heaven, and there is no hell. Therefore, in the absence of a real reply they resorted to ridicule and jeering mockery.

Those who procrastinated were influenced by the logic and the truth of what Paul said, but they were not prepared to act on the truth. They told Paul they wanted to hear him again.

But those who accepted the good news treasured the truth. Two of these are named by Luke. One was Dionysius, the Areopagite—that is, a member, one of the judges on the Council of Areopagus. The other, a woman named Damaris, was a person of excellent character, known favorably in the community. In addition to these, Luke grouped together an unspecified number of believers as "a number of others."

SUMMARY

As the Second Missionary Journey moved on through southeastern Europe, Paul focused on proving God was the God of the Scriptures, revealed through His Son Jesus Christ. Continued opposition from the Jews forced Paul to go on ahead of the rest of the party, ending up in the intellectually healthy but spiritually and morally poor city of Athens. There Paul came up against not Jews, nor the normal group of Gentiles he had previously ministered to, but he came in contact with some of the most learned and bright people to be found anywhere in the world at that time.

When Robert Owen, the notorious freethinker, visited Alexander Campbell to arrange the preliminaries for the great debate which was to follow, they walked about the farm and came to the family burying ground. "There is one advantage I have over the Christian," boasted Mr. Owen. "I am not afraid to die. Most Christians have fear in death, but if some few items of my business were settled, I would be perfectly willing to die at any moment."

"Well," replied Mr. Campbell, "you say you have no fear in death; have you any hope in death?" After a solemn pause, Mr. Owen answered soberly, "No."

"Then," said Mr. Campbell, pointing to an ox standing nearby, "you are on a level with that brute. He has fed till he is satisfied, and stands in the shade whisking off the flies, and has neither hope nor fear in death."

Paul challenged the Epicureans and Stoics of Athens with a religious belief of which they had never heard. Included in that Paul pointed to the certainty of the resurrection of the dead, to be followed with the judgment by the one true and living God.

(6 minutes)

Have group members share their responses to study guide item 14. Ask individuals the following questions:

1. "What can you do to prepare to address those who are highly educated?"

2. "What would your response be to those who reacted to your attempt to evangelize as the Athenians did?"

Select two or three items from the "Let's Review" section for review of this study.

Close the session with prayer asking God to help us have courage, creativity, and clarity in presenting the gospel of Jesus to the world around us.

Remind group members to complete study 10 before the next session.

Encourage individuals to take the time to fellowship together before they leave the session.

LET'S REVIEW

1. What was the charge brought against Paul at Thessalonica?

____

____

____

2. What was it that stirred Paul so deeply in Athens?

____

____

____

____

3. What unusual approach did Paul employ at Mars' Hill?

____

____

____

4. Why do you suppose Paul quoted Greek poets in his message?

____

____

____

5. Is there any similarity in the response at Athens and the attitude of intellectuals to God today?

____

____

____

6. Where or who is your mission field and how can you reach out to them?

____

____

____

STUDY 10

COMRADES OF THE CROSS

Paul gave his famous Mars' Hill address before the Council. But when he reached the climax of his message and referred to the resurrection of Jesus, he was greeted with derisive laughter. It was impossible for the Council to believe that this man and this strange religion could be a threat to Athens.

Our present study concerns the planting of the gospel in Corinth and Ephesus, two of the great cities of the Roman world. This study focuses on Paul's fellow laborers in the preaching of the good news. New workers appear, such as Aquila, Priscilla, Apollos, Gaius, and Aristarchus, along with Silas and Timothy who continue to be associated with Paul as comrades of the Cross.

As we disciple each other and work together in love, we will be more effective in sharing the gospel.

Study Objective

To look at the cooperation of the Early Church workers and model our relationships after this pattern.

What You Will Need

☐ Prepare a Bible character name tag for each group member.
☐ Duplicate enough copies of resources 10A, "Tentmaking Today," and 10B, "Ephesus Fact Sheet," for each individual.
☐ Locate and reuse resource 6B, "Paul's Journeys."
☐ An overhead projector.

Getting The Group's Attention

(All times are estimates. 8 minutes)

Divide the large group into two smaller groups. After the groups have been formed, place a Bible character name tag on the back of each group member. The point of this activity is to work together and help each individual discover his identity. To do so, have each person take a turn by standing up and turning around to show his identity. After being seated again these individuals are to ask questions of the group which would result in discovering their identities.

Possible questions are: "Where was I born?" and "In what time period did I live?"

After everyone has had a turn, bring the two groups together and ask, "How did it feel to help others discover who they were?" or "How did it feel to work together as a group toward a common goal?"

Transition Statement

Lecture
(2 minutes)

Summarize the background material concerning the city of Corinth provided in the parallel column. You may wish to enhance your presentation by reading through the "Corinth" section of a Bible dictionary.

Response
(2 minutes)

Have group members share their responses to study guide item 1.

Handout
(5 minutes)

Distribute a copy of resource 10A, "Tentmaking Today," to each individual. Have them read it over and discuss the possibilities available to them as tentmakers if they choose to pursue that avenue.

Corinth was the capital of Achaia, the southern province of Greece. It was a beautiful city situated on a narrow isthmus with a seaport on either side. The western seaport faced toward Rome, and the other at Cenchrea, 8 miles away, faced the East. Nero had a canal started across the isthmus, an early version of the Panama Canal; it was completed approximately 100 years ago. Corinth was noted for the exceptional beauty of its paintings, sculpture, and art forms. The finest bronze of the times was "Corinthian brass." As a thriving commercial center, the city boasted a population of some 400,000. And like most commercial centers, the population was a cross section of almost every level of life.

The moral quality of the city was the worst Paul had faced. Corinth had a reputation the world over for licentiousness and immorality. With all its classic beauty, the city seemed to have drawn within itself the dregs of all that made Sodom and Gomorrah a notorious place of sin.

1. What do you think it may have felt like to be a solitary minister in a city with the reputation of Corinth?

____

____

____

In Corinth, Paul faced what must be considered a grave crisis period in his life. He was alone, waiting for the arrival of Silas and Timothy. The opposition from his own people was probably the heaviest part of the burden he carried. He longed to win his fellow Jews to Christ, but his every attempt raised a storm of resistance. And now he faced, in Corinth, a city of such corruption that its name was a byword for evil. To "Corinthianize" was to plunge to the depths of all moral depravity.

2. Read Acts 18:1-4. Whom did Paul team up with in Corinth?

____

____

Why were these individuals in Corinth?

____

____

In these same verses we find the first reference to financial support of this missions endeavor. How did Paul support himself during this time?

____

____

3. What do the following passages teach us about Priscilla and Aquila? (Acts 18:2,18,19; Romans 16:3-5; 1 Corinthians 16:19).

____

____

____

____

The church in Corinth began in the synagogue where Paul went on the Sabbath days to share in discussions about the Scriptures. During the weekdays he worked at his trade. Luke does not tell us where Paul first met Aquila. It could have been at the synagogue or at his place of business. Aquila and his wife Priscilla were strongly drawn to Paul and invited him to make his home with them.

4. Read Acts 18:5,6 and record the impact that the arrival of Silas and Timothy had on Paul and the evangelistic effort in Corinth.

____

____

____

With his comrades in service, Silas, Timothy, Aquila, and Priscilla, Paul witnessed more vigorously than before to the Jews. But the indifference of the Jews now turned to animosity. They hurled insults and blasphemies at Paul and the good news he proclaimed. Feeling he had relieved himself of responsibility to the Jews, Paul shook his clothes, in the typical gesture of the times (Matthew 10:14), and declared that from this time on he would go to the Gentiles.

5. According to Acts 18:7,8, where did Paul go to proclaim the good news?

____

____

What was the result? ______________________________

____

____

This location was more accessible to Gentiles, and yet being near the synagogue, made it possible for Jews to attend also. The struggle came to a turning point with the conversion of Crispus, the chief ruler of the synagogue. On hearing this, many Corinthians believed and were baptized.

6. Paul felt he was at a point of decision concerning the future of his ministry in Corinth. At a time when he was emotionally spent, the Holy Spirit came and encouraged him with direction. Read Acts 18:9-11 and record the direction and result below.

____

____

____

Never had Paul faced a more difficult decision. He had worked hard with very little fruit to show for his labors. It seemed impossible to break through to the Corinthians. He wrote later in his epistle that he came to Corinth in weakness, and fear, and with much trembling (1 Corinthians 2:3). But the Lord promised Paul He would be with him.

AN UNEXPECTED HELPER

The proconsul (governor) Gallio was described as a pleasant, popular man. His brother Seneca was the famous philosopher and poet. Seneca wrote of Gallio, "Those who love him to the utmost, do not love him enough."

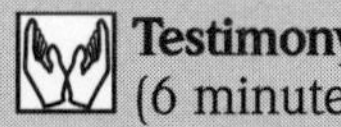
Testimony
(6 minutes)

Have someone share a time when the Lord used the testimony of someone else to lift his/her spirit.

Ask individuals the following questions:

1. "Why is it important to publicly share what the Lord has done?"

2. "In what ways is giving testimony a ministry to the Body?"

Discussion
(3 minutes)

Ask group members, "What means has God used to provide you clear direction regarding His will?"

7. As had happened everywhere else, the Early Church missionaries met resistance as their evangelistic thrust continued. Describe the events recorded in Acts 18:12-17, and reflect on the potential encouragement this event must have been for the infant church at Corinth.

____

____

____

It was unexpected help. In effect, Gallio had ruled that a person's religion was a matter of individual choice, and the Roman courts would not interfere as long as no crime was involved against society or the state. Gallio's ruling was an important victory for the tiny handful of believers.

Encouraged with this turn of events, Paul continued his work in Corinth for a while. Sensing the release of the Spirit, he bade the people of the church farewell and started off again.

8. Read Acts 18:18-22. It's apparent that the Second Missionary Journey is drawing to a close. Whom does Paul leave to lead the church in Corinth?

____

____

Where does Paul leave Priscilla and Aquila? _______________________

____

____

Luke records the fact that Paul had vowed a vow to the Lord. It is not revealed what the vow was all about, only this, that as a part of his consecration, Paul shaved his head before departing from Cenchrea. For reasons of his own, Paul separated himself to God in the manner of the Nazirites (Numbers 6:1-21). And this required that he return by way of Jerusalem in order to make his offering in accordance with Jewish law.

It must be noted that though Paul resisted all efforts to bring Gentiles under obligation to the Law, he scrupulously observed the commands of Moses.

Eventually, Paul reached Caesarea on the coast of Palestine. From there he went up to Jerusalem—the phrase "went up" means just that. From the coastal plain he ascended the hills of Judea to Jerusalem, located at an altitude of about 2,500 feet. Having reported to the church, he "went down" to Antioch, and thus his Second Missionary Journey was completed.

A NEW PARTNER

Alexandria was an important city on the coast of Egypt. It was the center of a large concentration of Jews. There, one of the finest schools of Judaism had been established. The stunning call of John to prepare for the coming Messiah had moved Apollos, a minister of the gospel who is introduced in Acts 18. With this limited revelation of Christ, he spoke out fervently in the synagogue.

9. Read Acts 18:24-28. List some of the facts revealed about Apollos.

____

____

____

Aquila and Priscilla quickly perceived Apollos' limited knowledge about the promised Messiah. Tactfully and privately, they led him into a deeper spiritual relationship with Jesus. Now this fervent man was further inspired. When he felt led to go in the direction of Corinth and Achaia, the brethren wrote letters of commendation.

The ending of the Second Missionary Journey and the beginning of the third are blended together in two brief verses (Acts 18:22,23). Paul spent "some time" with the believers in his home church at Antioch and then started out again. Apparently he followed the same land route that he had taken in the second journey—through Syria into Cilicia, through the Gates of Cilicia and back to the cities of Derbe, Lystra, Iconium, and Antioch in Pisidia. At length he came to Ephesus. Prior to this, the Holy Spirit had forbidden him to enter this region. Now the way was clear and, in the Spirit's time with the Spirit's blessing, he came to this capital city of Asia.

Ephesus was the city of greatest importance in Asia Minor. Its crowning glory was the Temple of Diana, one of the seven wonders of the world. In all the ancient world there was scarcely anything more magnificent than this great pagan temple. In front of the temple was a rude idol, said to have fallen from heaven. On the western slope of the city, the Greeks had built one of their largest amphitheaters, capable of holding some 24,000 people. There were four natural passes in the surrounding hills, and through these ran the roads that led to the six other cities mentioned in the Book of Revelation.

10. Read Acts 19:1-7. What seemed to be of utmost importance to Paul as he arrived in Ephesus?

____

____

____

How do these verses demonstrate that the baptism in the Holy Spirit is distinct from personal salvation?

____

____

The little band that formed the nucleus of believers in Ephesus had progressed no further than John's baptism of repentance. They were still awaiting the arrival of the Messiah and were unaware of the gift of the Holy Spirit. Paul now introduced them to the Messiah and taught them of the baptism in the Holy Spirit.

11. According to Acts 19:8-12, Paul's ministry once again faced opposition. How did the Holy Spirit lend credibility to Paul's ministry in Ephesus?

____

____

For the next 2 years, Paul engaged in intensive evangelism. He was assisted by the 12 Ephesian men plus Silas, Timothy, Gaius, Aristarchus, Aquila, and Priscilla. Ephesus was a center from which the Word was distributed. The seven churches of Asia (from Revelation 1-3) were probably formed during this extensive evangelistic effort. All of these cities were within easy reach of Ephesus.

12. Read Acts 19:13-22. How did the events in this passage validate Paul's authority and authenticity?

____

____

____

Once again we see something good coming from a negative situation. How did this affect those who practiced sorcery in Ephesus?

____

____

____

____

✎ **13. Read Acts 19:23-41 and respond to the following questions:**

What was the basis of the riot which occurred in Ephesus?___________________

____

____

____

What motivated the people who incited the riot?___________________

____

____

____

How was the riot resolved?___________________

____

____

____

When finally dispersed, one great fact remained—Paul and his comrades had planted the Cross in Ephesus and it was there to stay.

<table><tr><td>

SUMMARY

</td></tr></table>

Shortly after World War II, a church building that had suffered a direct hit during the bombing of London was renovated for use. The congregation had worked hard to get the building ready for the services. Everything looked lovely and in order. But the one thing they had not been able to accomplish was restoration of the power system for the organ. But these determined people were not to be defeated. While the organist played at the console, an individual behind the curtains worked the levers of a hand pump to provide power for the organ. It became a beautiful illustration of the fact that we are laborers together with God. The talented musician at the keyboard could have accomplished nothing were it not for the faithful, consistent efforts of the person working the pumps!

Paul knew that teamwork was essential to missions. It was never more evident than in Corinth and Ephesus. As the missionary flame spread out to these two cities, challenges and demands emerged that had not previously been encountered. Without the efforts and support of each of the ministerial associates and new converts there probably would have been greater discouragement, not to mention the inability to get the good news of Jesus to as many faraway places. If anyone had a temptation to focus on his accomplishments, it would have been Paul, yet we see him summing up the reality of what took place on his second journey. "I planted the seed, Apollos watered it, but God made it grow" (1 Corinthians 3:6, NIV). The work of God is the work of many hands. A spirit of cooperation produces rich spiritual dividends.

Response
(2 minutes)

Have group members share their responses to study guide item 13.

Discussion
(3 minutes)

Ask individuals, "In what ways does today's society strike back at the positive changes brought about by effective Christian witness?"

Testimony
(2 minutes)

Have individuals share times when seeming persecution actually resulted in multiplied ministry opportunities.

1. Who made up the ministry team in Corinth?

____

____

____

2. What events brought Paul's ministry to a close in Corinth?

____

____

____

____

3. How did Paul's Second Missionary Journey conclude?

____

____

____

____

4. How and where did Paul's Third Missionary Journey begin?

____

____

____

5. What were the highlights of Paul's great victory in Ephesus?

____

____

____

____

6. How did teamwork affect Paul's ministry at the end of the Second Missionary Journey and the beginning of the Third Missionary Journey?

____

____

____

____

Review
(4 minutes)
Select two or three items from the "Let's Review" section to review this study.

Closing Prayer
(2 minutes)
Close in prayer asking God to help group members learn to work together toward the common goal of winning the world for Christ.

Preparing For Next Session
Remind individuals to complete study 11 before the next session.

Discussion
(3 minutes)
Begin discussing possible study topics to be explored after the completion of *Acts: To The Ends Of The Earth*.
You may wish to consider another study from the *Spiritual Discovery Series*. For a complete listing of available topics, see your *Radiant Life* order form or supplier.

Group Fellowship
(5 minutes)
Invite individuals to share the refreshments brought to the session.

Study Objective

To observe Paul's commitment to his spiritual goal and make a similar commitment to move forward in Christ.

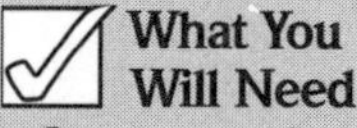

What You Will Need

☐ Locate and reuse resource 6B, "Paul's Journeys."
☐ An overhead projector.
☐ Enough copies of resources 11A, "Bringing It Home," and 11B, "Holy Ground," for each group member.

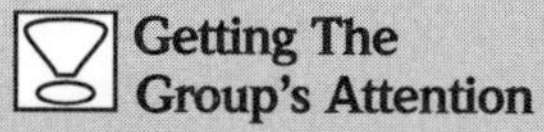

Getting The Group's Attention

(All times are estimates. 8 minutes)

Distribute a copy of resource 11A, "Bringing It Home," to each group member. Give them 3 minutes to complete the work sheet.

Have individuals share their responses with the group.

Conclude by having individuals pair with another person and pray for supernatural strength to be courageous in witnessing to others.

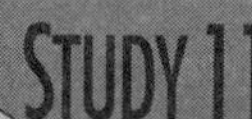

JOURNEY INTO DANGER

For a long time, Paul had desired to go to Rome and from there penetrate even more deeply into the Roman Empire. But before he could fulfill this desire, there was need to go first to Macedonia and then to Jerusalem.

Luke does not state the reasons why Paul undertook this particular journey before going to Rome. Several possibilities emerge as the story unfolds. For quite some time the Gentile believers had been gathering funds to assist the impoverished believers in Jerusalem. Difficult times had come to the people in the first church. Paul felt that a manifestation of love and concern on the part of the Gentile believers could be used by the Holy Spirit to bring healing between Jewish and Gentile churches.

Transition Statement

Our Christian commitment includes dedication to follow God's will regardless of the cost.

Paul recognized that the situation in Ephesus was replete with danger—for the Church, as well as for himself. The crowd had been dispersed; Gaius and Aristarchus had been released; but the peril remained. The hostility had been directed mostly against the apostle and for this reason he decided to depart rather than precipitate mob violence which would injure the work. But more than this, the work in Ephesus was now well established and Paul could safely leave it in the care of the elders.

1. Read Acts 20:1-6. Recount the travels of Paul after leaving Ephesus.

____

____

____

Paul remained in Greece ministering to the church at Corinth for 3 months.

There was a heavy weight upon Paul's heart concerning the church in Corinth. The licentious spirit of Corinth had crept into the church. A flagrant instance of incest existed among members of the church unrebuked. Paul felt it an absolute necessity to go and seek to help the believers in this time of difficulty.

2. According to 2 Corinthians 7:2-16, what was the condition of the church in Corinth when Paul arrived?

____

____

During the winter months in Corinth, Paul found the time to write one of his epistles—the Book of Romans.

Apparently it was Paul's plan to take the offerings the Gentile believers had gathered and deliver them in person to the church in Jerusalem. In addition to the offering, each church had chosen a special messenger to represent the local congregation. These chosen ones formed Paul's party and accompanied him to Jerusalem.

3. Read Acts 20:4. List the names of the seven men who accompanied Paul to Jerusalem.

____

____

____

Three of these men were from the Macedonian churches, and four came from the congregations in Asia Minor. It seems clear that each of the Gentile congregations had given generously.

4. Refer back to Acts 2:42-47 and 4:32-37. According to these passages, how do you think the church in Jerusalem responded when Gentile representatives set out to deliver generous contributions from their respective congregations?

____

____

____

Overhead
(1 minute)

Place the overhead transparency of resource 6B, "Paul's Journeys," on the overhead projector and continue to trace the route of Paul's final journey as you go through this study.

Response
(3 minutes)

Have individuals share their responses to study guide item 2.

Discussion
(3 minutes)

Ask group members the following questions:

1. "According to Romans 15:23-27, what was the reason for donating the money to the Jews?"

2. "In the overall scope of the Early Church, what is the significance of the offerings contributed by the Gentiles to the Jerusalem church?"

Discussion
(3 minutes)

Ask individuals, "Why do you suppose all the persecution was focused on Paul when there were other apostles and leaders?"

Testimony
(4 minutes)

Have 1 or 2 group members share of a meeting that lasted a long time, yet no one really wanted to leave.

Response
(4 minutes)

Have individuals share their responses to study guide item 6. Ask group members, "What axiom does Paul seem to be supporting here by commending them to keep up the good work of God?"

As the group set out to deliver the contributions, it was discovered that certain fanatical Jews were waiting for Paul to murder him, and probably to seize the offerings he carried to Jerusalem. In response certain members of Paul's party went by ship according to the original plan, while Paul and several others traveled by land through Macedonia. They planned to meet in Troas and then proceed together to Jerusalem.

Luke joined Paul at Philippi as the entry of "we" in Acts 20:6 indicates. It must have been a difficult journey to Troas, for it took 5 days, when normally the trip took about 48 hours. Paul and his companions waited in Troas for a ship going toward Syria. During this time they shared rich fellowship with the believers in the city.

5. Read Acts 20:7-12. What does the story of Eutychus reveal about Paul's love for the people at Troas?

____

____

____

A heartwarming picture is given of the final fellowship meeting in Troas. It was the first day of the week and the disciples met for Communion. Time was unimportant. Testimonies, prayers, and Paul's sermon continued the meeting to the midnight hour. Luke says that there were many lights and, quite likely, the room was poorly ventilated. Young Eutychus sat in a windowsill on an upper level. Overcome by the warm air and weariness, the young man fell to his death. Paul bent over the lad, embraced him, praying the Lord to restore life to him. It must have been a thrilling moment to see the boy's eyes open, and then to announce to all that life had returned to Eutychus.

The sense of the Lord's presence in this marvelous answer to prayer surely must have brought new strength to Paul and his companions.

DANGER SIGNALS

Paul was determined to get to Jerusalem for the Feast of Pentecost (Acts 20:13-16). To do this, he was obliged to keep moving even when he would have liked to remain longer with the believers at the various ports of call. He realized that there would not be time for him to go to Ephesus so he sent word ahead, requesting the Ephesian elders to come and meet him at the seaport Miletus. Paul's earnest message in the presence of the Ephesian elders is warm with the love of Christ and with inspiring exhortation to faithfulness.

6. On his way home, Paul shared a message with the elders from Ephesus in Acts 20:17-38. It was an emotional meeting for both sides. Consider the main points of Paul's farewell message to these men and discuss why it was such an emotional time for all involved.

____

____

____

____

First, Paul reviewed the blessed experiences of the past, reminding them how he had lived with and ministered to them. The life of the apostle had been a vivid illustration of Christianity. Then, he pointed forward to the future and told them that repeatedly the Holy Spirit warned that bonds and afflictions awaited him in Jerusalem. But he assured them that none of these things could dissuade him. Paul was unalterably committed to the cause of Christ. He exhorted the elders to be true to God. They held their positions as overseers under God. They were to keep watch over themselves and their flock. Finally, Paul commended them to the loving care of God. He urged them to continue to give of themselves to the work of God because it's better to give than to receive.

The last scene of Paul and the Ephesian elders kneeling, embracing, and praying together is a beautiful demonstration of the loving fellowship of God's children. It was a tearful scene.

7. Read Acts 21:1-15. Paul and his companions continued toward Jerusalem via the sea. Where did they stop? Describe what happened in each place.

____

____

____

____

Compare this passage with Acts 16:6-10. What conditions are similar? _____________

____

What conditions are different? _______________________________________

____

Do you believe Paul was disobedient to the Holy Spirit? Why or why not? ___________

____

Luke emphasizes that all, including himself, begged Paul to abandon his thought of going to Jerusalem. Paul was moved by their concern, but he remained adamant in his resolution. And though they could not comprehend, they yielded, trusting the Lord's will to be done. The party left Philip's house and went up to Jerusalem.

THE PERILOUS PLAN

James and the brethren warmly welcomed Paul and his companions. Each of the Gentile representatives was presented to the apostles and elders. It could well be that, as they were identified, they presented their love gifts on behalf of the Gentile churches who had sent them. There were tears of joy and expressions of thanksgiving to God for these evidences of loving Christian fellowship.

Paul related in detail the fruit of their ministry, and how the Holy Spirit had manifested himself in signs and wonders. The report stirred the church and they offered praises to God.

But Paul quickly learned that the elders were troubled by his presence in Jerusalem. They pointed out to him that there were two parties among the Jerusalem believers. One group was in sympathy with Paul and his ministry among the Gentiles. The other group, the Judaizers, felt that Paul was in serious error. This was not news to Paul! He had already suffered greatly at the hands of these fanatical Judaizers.

8. What false accusation was leveled against Paul in Acts 21:17-25?

____

____

____

Paul honored the Law and was most careful in observing the commands of Moses. But he insisted that salvation was by grace through faith, not by works of obedience to the Law. He did not consider circumcision, a sign given to the Jews, essential to the salvation of Gentiles. Paul had witnessed the miracle of regeneration in many Gentiles and he knew it to be a genuine work of the Holy Spirit.

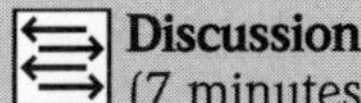

(7 minutes)

Have individuals share their responses to study guide item 7. Then ask the following questions:

1. "How does God use individuals to speak to us about events or circumstances in our lives?"

2. "What is our responsibility to God when someone gives us a 'word from God'?"

(3 minutes)

Have group members share their responses to study guide item 8.

✎ **9. Paul was willing to go the extra mile personally, in reconciling with the Judaizers. What did he choose to do to show this? (Acts 21:26).**

The apostles and elders took the position that Paul was misunderstood and misrepresented; however, they pointed out that the hostility against him was extreme and exceedingly dangerous. It was important that he move with great caution and, if possible, demonstrate to the Judaizers that he was indeed a faithful son of the Law. In their eyes they were not suggesting a compromise on the Jerusalem decision; they, in fact, reaffirmed that historic document.

Four men in the Jerusalem church had taken on themselves a Nazirite vow. As poor men, they were having difficulty in raising the necessary temple fees to complete their vows. The brethren asked Paul to demonstrate to the Judaizers his faithfulness to the Law. Paul agreed.

It seemed an ironic twist of fate that the perilous plan Paul followed came so close to success. The 7 days of purification had almost ended when Asian Jews recognized Paul. It was not the Judaizers, but non-Christian Jews who started the riot.

✎ **10. Continue reading Acts 21:27-36. What happened to Paul once he was recognized by Jews in the city?**

Who saved his life? _______________________

How did Paul's experience parallel Jesus' as recorded in Luke 22:66 to 23:25?

Only a few days before this, Paul had been seen walking the streets of Jerusalem with a Gentile, Trophimus the Ephesian. Now the Jews saw Paul in the temple with four men, and they were convinced that Paul had profaned the temple by bringing Trophimus into the inner court of the temple. To the Jewish mind there was no greater desecration possible.

Gentiles were permitted to enter the outer court of the temple, but the inner court was for Jews only. Warning signs were placed conspicuously, plainly informing all non-Jews that entrance into the inner court was punishable by death.

At the northwest corner of the temple area there stood the Tower of Antonia. Roman soldiers were quartered there as a peacekeeping force in Jerusalem. As Paul and the soldiers struggled up the stairs toward the Tower, Paul, in excellent Greek, asked the Roman tribune for permission to speak to the people. Permission was granted. The mob listened attentively as Paul spoke to them in Hebrew.

✎ **11. Read Acts 21:37 to 22:22. At what point did the crowd revolt against Paul's message?**

✎ **12. As recorded in Acts 22:22-29, what was Paul's advantage through his Roman citizenship?**

____

____

____

Paul escaped the horrible torture of the Roman whipping post, but he was still a prisoner. The Roman tribune, Claudius Lysias, was puzzled because he did not know on what charges the prisoner was to be booked. It was a serious position for him because the prisoner, a Roman citizen, had apparently not violated Roman law. Yet if Paul were released, the mob would surely kill him. It occurred to the tribune that it might be well to oblige the Sanhedrin to state the charges against Paul. Therefore, he ordered the Sanhedrin to meet the following morning.

✎ **13. Read Acts 22:30 through 23:10. What did the Roman commander decide to do to determine what crime Paul should be charged with?**

____

What plan did Paul use to throw this group into chaos?

____

____

It was quite clear to Paul that a fair trial before this body was an impossibility. He had scarcely begun his address when he was cruelly slapped by the command of the high priest. The hostility was quite apparent. It was a hopeless situation. Paul split the hearing wide open with an unusual stratagem. Probably Paul had witnessed many heated debates between the materialistic Sadducees and the conservative Pharisees. So Paul claimed he was being tried for something that the two groups were in disagreement over. This divided the Council.

Was this just an inexcusable, clever trick on Paul's part? Not really. Paul was being tried on the charge of heresy. Part of the alleged heresy of the followers of the Way was their faith in the crucified, risen Jesus as the promised Messiah. The dissension which broke out became so violent that the Roman soldiers had to rescue Paul and carry him back to the military barracks.

In coming to Jerusalem, Paul had indeed journeyed directly into the most perilous danger.

SUMMARY

When the famous Disraeli served as prime minister in Great Britain, he was once contemptuously referred to as a Jew. He replied to the member of Parliament who made the remark, "My lord, you accuse me of being a Jew. I am proud to answer to the name, and I would remind you sir, that one half of Christendom worships a Jew, and the other half reveres a Jewess. And I would also remind you that my forefathers were worshiping the one true and living God while yours were naked savages in the woods of Britain."

It is certainly no secret that the apostle Paul was called to carry the gospel to the Gentiles. But Paul was always careful to identify Christianity with the revelation of God to Israel. He spoke of his faith in conjunction with "the God of our fathers." And though he did not require it of new converts, in his personal life he was always careful that he measured up to the Law, so that he might not offend any.

As we conclude studying Paul's three missionary journeys, it is evident that the Holy Spirit's anointing, empowerment, and direction were constant companions. There were many victories, but not without struggles and challenges, mostly from the hands of the Jews. God's chosen people, Paul's own people, were the very ones who brought about the most grief during this time and ultimately the end of his ministry on this earth.

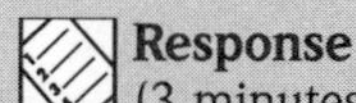

Response
(3 minutes)
Have group members share their responses to study guide item 12.

Response
(3 minutes)
Have individuals share their responses to study guide item 13.

Review
(5 minutes)

Select two or three items from the "Let's Review" section to review the study.

Closing Prayer
(2 minutes)

Close in prayer asking God to help us to grow in determination and character so that we can be strong in the face of adversity.

Preparing For Next Session

Remind group members to complete study 12 before the next session. Ask an individual to prepare a report on King Agrippa II.

Discussion
(3 minutes)

Continue discussing possible study topics to be explored after the completion of *Acts: To The Ends Of The Earth*.

You may wish to consider another study from the **Spiritual Discovery Series**. For a complete listing of available topics, see your *Radiant Life* order form or contact your local supplier.

Group Fellowship
(5 minutes)

Invite group members to share in the refreshments while fellowshipping together.

LET'S REVIEW

1. Why was Paul obliged to take the longer land route through Macedonia instead of taking a ship from Corinth?

____

____

____

2. What happened when Paul preached at Troas?

____

____

____

3. How was Paul dramatically warned at Caesarea not to go to Jerusalem?

____

____

____

____

4. Why was Paul mobbed and arrested in the temple?

____

____

____

5. What other situation involving the Sanhedrin and the Roman authorities does this event remind you of?

____

____

____

6. When warned of impending dangers in Jerusalem, what was Paul's response? How can you begin to answer in this same manner when you face adversity?

____

____

____

____

STUDY 12

MINISTER EXTRAORDINARY

As we discovered in the last study, the Roman captain's hopes to discover the cause of all the trouble were short-lived. The Sanhedrin was a hostile court. Paul sensed that these men were determined to do away with him. He appealed to the Pharisees for their help, declaring that he was on trial for his faith in the resurrection. Paul's statement touched a sore point between the Sadducees and the Pharisees. They turned on each other. The feelings grew so intense that the Roman captain had to intervene in order to save Paul's life.

However, Paul was not abandoned by God. The attempts of his enemies to destroy him and Christianity were divinely overruled by God. It was God's design to bring the gospel message to the outstanding rulers in Palestine, and eventually to carry the good news to Rome itself.

Paul sets an example of tenacity in Christian witness for Christians to model.

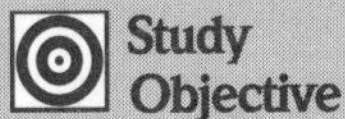

Study Objective

To understand the inner strength and wisdom of Paul and dedicate ourselves to growing in the Lord so that we may present this same type of example.

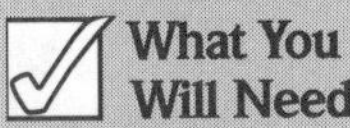

What You Will Need

☐ Enough copies of resources 12A, "Sacrilege!" and 12B, "Paul's Defense," for each group member.

☐ Ask an individual to prepare a report on King Agrippa II.

Getting The Group's Attention

(All times are estimates. 7 minutes)

Distribute a copy of resource 12A, "Sacrilege!" to each group member. Give individuals 4 minutes to complete the work sheet. Have group members share their "defenses."

Transition Statement

Paul's appearance before the Sanhedrin ended in a riot. It was necessary for the Roman captain to use force to rescue Paul from the hands of these angry religious leaders. Paul was returned to the military barracks in the Tower of Antonia. The Roman captain was still confused as to why riots erupted every time Paul appeared before the Jews.

Paul was exhausted from the continued pressure of fierce opposition. Twice he had narrowly escaped death; he knew that the threat of death constantly rested upon him. He may well have despaired that his desire to bring healing between Jews and Gentiles had now been destroyed by the riot in the temple and in the Sanhedrin. It is possible that he felt a keen sense of disappointment at the apparent frustration of his plans to go to Rome.

1. Read Acts 23:11. In the midst of confusion, danger, and confinement, what happened to reassure Paul that his life would be spared?

____

____

____

2. Read Acts 23:12-35. Describe the Jewish conspiracy against Paul.

____

____

____

____

How did Paul avoid this attempt on his life? _______________________

____

____

Where was Paul taken and why?_______________________________

____

____

____

But divine providence intervened. The willingness of the Roman officer to seriously consider the boy's story indicated the influence of Paul's godly character, and the Roman's knowledge of the desperate nature of the Jewish zealots.

God used unholy people to bring about holy results. Paul was scheduled by the Holy Spirit to witness for Christ to some very influential, highly placed people.

History describes Felix as a man both lustful and cruel. Tacitus, a Roman historian, wrote that Felix exercised the powers of a king in the spirit of a slave. Maclaren makes this perceptive contrast, "Beggars on horseback and princes walking are bad enough, but scoundrels as magistrates and saints as prisoners on trial are worse still."

Paul's first hearing before Felix occurred about 5 days after his arrival in Caesarea. The delegation from Jerusalem, headed by the high priest Ananias, included legal counsel in the person of Tertullus, a professional lawyer. As a Roman, Tertullus had wide knowledge of the Roman courts and procedures. It was expected that he would be able to effectively prosecute the case against Paul.

The entire situation was extremely distasteful to the high priest and the members of the Sanhedrin. They were in the uncomfortable position of being obliged to request a despised Gentile to release to them one whom they considered to be an apostate Jew.

Tertullus began his presentation with elaborate compliments to Felix. He lauded the governor for the peace he had brought to the province. It is true that Felix had successfully captured and destroyed some robber bands who had terrorized the community. But in the main, the governor's administration was exceptionally corrupt. Two years later, Felix faced charges before Nero and was removed from his office.

✎ **3. Look up Acts 24:1-9. Of what did the Jerusalem group accuse Paul?**

____

____

____

____

The high priest and the members of the Sanhedrin present at the trial gave their endorsement to all that Tertullus had said, and, in so doing, perjured themselves.

✎ **4. Tertullus brought a convincing argument, slanted to sway the Romans against Paul. In Acts 24:10-21 Paul is given the opportunity to defend himself. Summarize his speech.**

____

____

____

____

Paul's opening remarks were courteous, sincere, but without attempts at flattery. He quite correctly pointed out that Felix had for many years served as a judge over the nation of Israel and therefore was well qualified to understand the issues and render wise judgment.

He invited Felix to consider the facts concerning each of the three charges made by Tertullus. (1) The charge of insurrection was ridiculous because Paul had been in Jerusalem only a few days. In the brief time he had been in Jerusalem he had not engaged in any public or private debate. (2) Paul confessed that he was a follower of "the Way," but that this was not heresy. Christianity was the fulfillment of the sacred promises God had made to the fathers of Israel. Paul declared that he worshiped the God of his fathers. How then could he be called a heretic? (3) As to the charge of desecration, this was unthinkable, and Paul directly denied the complaint. He was in the temple obediently fulfilling holy vows when Asian Jews assaulted him. They were the ones who had desecrated the temple. Paul contended that he had a right to face those who accused him of profaning the temple. Why were they not in court to press their charge?

✎ **5. How did Felix respond according to Acts 24:22,23?**

____

____

____

____

He did this even though he had Lysias' report in his possession. But Felix had yet another reason. He had learned that Paul, with others, had brought a large sum of money to Jerusalem. It appears that Felix thought Paul had wealthy friends who would gladly pay a large bribe to effect Paul's release.

Response
(3 minutes)
Have individuals share their responses to study guide item 3.

Lecture
(3 minutes)
Give a copy of resource 12B, "Paul's Defense," to each individual. Use this resource to assist you in presenting the material in the parallel column concerning Paul's speech before Felix.

Response
(2 minutes)
Have group members share their responses to study guide item 5.

For 2 years Paul had been held in protective custody. During this time, he had appeared privately before Felix and his Jewish wife Drusilla.

6. What did Paul share in his meetings with Felix and Drusilla? (Acts 24:24-26).

____

____

____

____

How did Felix react to Paul's discourse?

____

____

It is difficult to ascertain Drusilla's attitude toward Paul. Quite likely, as a Jewess, her sympathies would be with the high priest in his accusations against Paul. Possibly, as some scholars believe, Paul was held in prison at her insistence. History records the fact that Drusilla and her only child perished in Pompeii in the awful eruption of Vesuvius, A.D. 79.

At the private hearing, Felix trembled, but he did not repent. As time went on, Felix became more and more interested in a bribe, and less and less interested in righteousness. At the end of 2 years Nero removed Felix from office and appointed Porcius Festus in his place.

7. Read Acts 25:1-9. What happened upon the arrival of a new governor?

____

____

____

What does such severe reaction by the Jewish people after 2 long years reveal about Paul's impact on his society?

____

____

____

From all that can be learned, Festus came to office with a sincere desire to establish a good administration. Soon after taking office, he went to Jerusalem to gain the good will of the Jewish leaders. They tried to take advantage of what appeared to be an excellent opportunity. Festus was new in office, but he was too experienced not to sense that a scheme was involved.

Nothing new was introduced in the hearing. Luke summarized the new trial saying that the Jews gave many nasty complaints against Paul, which they could not prove.

Festus listened carefully to the complaints and the defense. It was clear that Paul was innocent of any crime against Rome. The real charges against Paul were related to Jewish customs. It seemed to Festus that an equitable manner of resolving the case would be to return Paul to the Sanhedrin who had jurisdiction in religious matters. As an assurance of fair treatment, Festus offered to preside at the trial. Possibly, he hoped that in this way he would please the Jews and, at the same time, guarantee the rights of Paul as a Roman citizen.

8. Read Acts 25:10-12. What was Paul's reaction to Festus' suggestion? And how did Festus respond in turn?

____

____

____

____

This came as a dramatic, unexpected climax to the trial. Though it seemed to come with surprising suddenness, undoubtedly Paul had considered this move for a long time. In effect, Paul was standing on his Roman citizenship again. He knew he had done no wrong to the Jews and was demanding that be recognized.

It was a tense moment for Festus. His legal advisers pointed out that Paul was properly exercising his rights as a citizen. The hearing ended with Festus' pronouncement that Paul would get his request.

In a sense, the case was still a problem to Porcius Festus. He was responsible to send to Caesar a detailed brief outlining the charges against Paul. The preparation of such a brief was now quite complicated for Festus. As a Roman citizen, Paul had not committed a crime against Rome. And further, Rome had little or no interest in the alleged violations against Jewish religious laws. It reflected against Festus' ability as an administrator to have this case appealed to Rome.

9. According to Acts 25:13, who arrived on the scene?

____

____

____

King Agrippa II was the son of Herod Agrippa I, who had executed the apostle James and imprisoned the apostle Peter. At the time of his father's terrible death (Acts 12:2-23), Agrippa II was regarded as being too young to receive the kingdom, but in due time he had risen to power. He was of Jewish blood, a descendant of the Maccabean priest-kings. But, he was regarded as a weak, sensual, pleasure-loving puppet of Rome. He had married his own sister, Bernice, and their marriage was a scandalous, incestuous affair. King Agrippa II was pleased to review Paul's case. Festus opened the session by briefing all present on the background, and Paul was given opportunity to speak for himself.

10. Describe Festus' dilemma as recorded in Acts 25:14-27.

____

____

____

____

11. Paul was given the unexpected opportunity to speak directly to King Agrippa. Read Acts 26:1-24. What did Paul include in the presentation of his defense?

____

____

(5 minutes)
Have the individual who has prepared the report on King Agrippa II give the presentation. Allow 2 minutes for questions from other group members following the report.

(5 minutes)
Read Acts 25:14-21, 24-27. Ask group members the following questions:

1. "Although Festus did not think he could release Paul, what seems to be his personal evaluation of the case?"

2. "How is this a precursor to current separation of church and government laws?"

Paul showed wisdom by beginning his defense by complimenting King Agrippa on his familiarity with Jewish customs and controversies. His speech is a moving, eloquent testimony to the grace of God. He shares from his heart the meaning of his life and ministry. He was interrupted by Festus who simply could not understand Paul's theology. He accused Paul of having such great learning that it was driving him insane.

In a surprising move, Paul appealed directly to King Agrippa asking if he believed in the prophets. He then answered for the stunned king stating that he knew he did.

12. In Acts 26:28,29, what was Agrippa's response to Paul's message?

____

____

____

____

How did Paul respond to Agrippa?

____

____

____

Most scholars believe that Agrippa's answer was intended to be devastating sarcasm. Probably, the court burst into laughter at this clever reply. But the apostle had the last word.

13. Read Acts 26:30-32. What private opinion did Festus and King Agrippa share concerning Paul's fate?

____

____

____

____

SUMMARY

Fanny Crosby's eyesight was destroyed when she was 6 weeks old. She lived some 90 years in the world of blindness. Lesser misfortunes have devastated others, but not Fanny Crosby. At the age of 12 she wrote, "Oh, what a happy soul am I/Even though I cannot see. I am resolved that in this world contented I shall be. How many blessings I enjoy/That other people don't. To weep and sigh because I'm blind/I cannot, and I won't."

She committed to memory the Psalms, the Proverbs, and the four Gospels. Out of this rich treasury of the Word there flowed a stream of gospel songs which have blessed the world. Her living Lord turned her troubles into channels of blessing.

Fanny Crosby reminds one of the apostle Paul. As he came to the end of his ministry, with the forces that opposed him seemingly gaining the upper hand, Paul used every opportunity to gain victory instead of defeat. Though this may not have been the way Paul would have guessed that he would have audiences with royalty, the imprisonment would eventually take him to Rome. Though the forces of evil were doing their best to destroy the work of God, they hadn't bargained on a fully committed, Holy Spirit filled messenger who valued nothing but the chance to testify for his Lord and Savior. Paul would use his chains and future trial in Rome to spread the gospel even deeper into Europe.

LET'S REVIEW

1. What new plot was made against Paul's life?

____

____

____

2. How was the death plot discovered?

____

____

____

3. Why didn't Felix release Paul after the hearing?

____

____

____

4. Who replaced Felix as governor?

____

____

____

5. Why did Paul appeal his case to Caesar?

____

____

____

6. From whom did Festus seek counsel concerning Paul?

____

____

____

7. How can you develop your inner spiritual strength so that you are prepared to answer questions or charges in the face of adversity?

____

____

____

Review
(5 minutes)
Select two or three items from the "Let's Review" section to review the study.

Closing Prayer
(2 minutes)
Close with a prayer for the help of the Spirit to grow strong in our conviction of the saving power of Jesus Christ.

Preparing For Next Session
Remind individuals to complete study 13 before the next session. Ask an individual to prepare a report on the period of Paul's life following the end of the Book of Acts.

Discussion
(3 minutes)
Make a decision regarding the next study topic to be explored after the completion of *Acts: To The Ends Of The Earth*.
Get a commitment from group members so that the proper number of study guides may be ordered for the next session.

Group Fellowship
(5 minutes)
Encourage group members to share together in fellowship and refreshments.

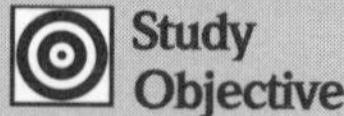

Study Objective

To view Christian character in action and seek to live a life of integrity.

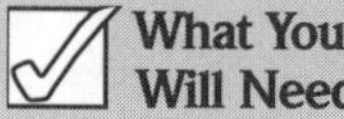

What You Will Need

- ☐ Bring in several board games.
- ☐ Locate and reuse resource 6B, "Paul's Journeys."
- ☐ An overhead projector.
- ☐ Duplicate enough copies of resource 13A, "A Time Line Of Paul," for each group member.
- ☐ Ask an individual to make a report on the period of Paul's life following the end of the Book of Acts.

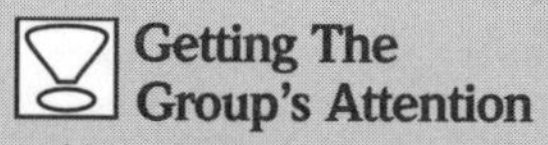

Getting The Group's Attention

(All times are estimates. 5 minutes)

Divide the group into as many groups as you have games. Have individuals begin to play the games but have them ignore the primary obstacle. (i.e., If a spinner is used to determine how many spaces to move, remove the spinner and have them just move the pieces as they wish. If an activity is required to gain a reward, eliminate that activity and grant the reward. If mental deduction is required to solve something, provide the elements that would have to be figured out.)

Give the groups 3 minutes to play. Ask individuals, "How do these adjusted games demonstrate what life would be like without its challenges?"

STUDY 13

THE UNCEASING WITNESS

Paul's witness to his fellow countrymen and to the rulers of Palestine ended with his appeal to Caesar. Felix, Festus, King Agrippa II, Drusilla, and Queen Bernice each heard the dynamic story of Christ from the lips of the apostle. The exercise of his right as a Roman citizen in appealing his case to Caesar opened an entirely new chapter in Paul's life.

Luke ends the Book of Acts by reporting Paul's 2-year period of ministry in the imperial city. During this time, Paul wrote the letters to the Philippians, the Colossians, Philemon, and possibly the letter to the Ephesians.

Paul's zeal in soul winning flamed in spite of chains and an everpresent Roman guard. Members of Caesar's household were numbered among the converts. No doubt, Paul's example inspired boldness and courage in the hearts of the Christians in Rome. Through his letters, Paul's ministry reached far beyond Rome to the churches of Asia Minor and Greece.

Transition Statement

Personal integrity and character will provide opportunities for effective ministry.

INTO THE STORM

Paul's life had been filled with many exciting, dangerous experiences. It would have been impossible for him to have foreseen the dramatic experiences before him. A partial list of his amazing adventures includes perils by land and by sea.

1. Read 2 Corinthians 11:23-27 and list below the dangers Paul had faced in life to that point.

____

____

____

From Caesarea, Paul began the long voyage to Rome.

2. Read Acts 27:1-8. Who traveled with Paul on the trip and how was Paul treated?

____

____

____

Travel by sea in Paul's day was primitive and risky. The mariners of those times knew nothing of the navigational aids available to modern sea travel, such as: (1) The compass by which the true north can be determined; (2) the sextant which makes it possible to compute the ship's position; and (3) the ship's log by which the rate of the ship's speed is established. As a consequence, the Roman sailing vessels rarely sailed beyond sight of land, whether the mainland or island. This limited their travel plans to favorable winds and favorable weather. When winter came with its stormy gales and long, black nights, the ships generally remained in port. This meant that most travel by sea was suspended from late fall (November) to early spring (March).

It seems that Paul's voyage to Rome did not get started until the travel season was nearing its close. They had not proceeded very far until Luke noted that sailing was dangerous. He pinpointed the fact that the fast during the Day of Atonement was now past (i.e., the 10th day of October). The delay in getting started may have been occasioned by the difficulty in finding a westbound ship of sufficient size to take the large group of prisoners and soldiers that formed the party. Paul and his fellow prisoners were under the constant guard of a detachment of Roman soldiers commanded by the centurion Julius.

As we have noted, progress was very slow. It was early October by the time the ship reached Myra, on the central coast of Asia Minor. There the entire party was transferred to a large Alexandrian grain ship. It was one of a fleet of vessels which plied between Alexandria in Egypt and Italy, carrying precious food grain to Rome. But this ship too, proved to be disappointingly slow. Many days later, having sailed southward from Cnidus, they arrived at a port called Fair Havens on the southern side of Crete. It was now well past the middle of October.

3. According to Acts 27:10-12, what did Paul encourage those in charge to do concerning their travel plans?

____

____

What did the centurion and pilot decide to do and why?

____

Response
(3 minutes)

Have group members share their responses to study guide item 1.

Overhead
(3 minutes)

Place overhead transparency of resource 6B, "Paul's Journeys," on the overhead projector. Use this map to trace Paul's travels as outlined in the parallel column.

In their minds there was no reason to listen to a prisoner. The reason for their decision seemed to justify it.

✎ 4. Continue reading in Acts 27, verses 13-20. What happened next and how did the ship's crew handle the situation?

____

____

____

____

All human expectation of surviving the storm was gone. It was then that Paul received a special visitation from the Lord.

✎ 5. Read Acts 27:21-26. What message did God give Paul for his and the other passengers' benefit?

____

____

____

God was telling Paul He had ordained him for further work. The good news was to be heralded before Caesar. God made a promise to Paul that night. Paul did not know exactly where the ship would end up, but he was assured safety. His faith was radiant with confidence and contagious.

But the storm continued to howl and the ship pitched on the wild waters for a total of 14 days.

✎ 6. Read Acts 27:27-30. In spite of the earlier assurance of Paul, what was the attitude and action of the sailors?

____

____

____

____

✎ 7. Read Acts 27:31-41. How was Paul's authority demonstrated in this situation?

____

____

____

It is interesting to note that, suddenly, Paul the prisoner took command. All aboard ship looked to him and drew from his confident faith the courage to believe. His conviction brought inspiration and strength to the 276 persons aboard.

In the early morning, as the boat began to fall apart under the relentless power of the sea, the sailors tried desperately to beach the ship.

A new danger then threatened Paul and his companions. According to Roman law, if a prisoner escaped, the guard's life was forfeited. Once again, God miraculously intervened on Paul's behalf.

Response
(3 minutes)

Have individuals share their responses to study guide item 4.

Discussion
(5 minutes)

Have group members share their responses to study guide item 5.

Ask individuals the following questions:

1. "Why do you think the commander and others were willing to listen to Paul this time?"

2. "Whom do you turn to when life's travels become rough? Why?"

Response
(3 minutes)

Have group members share their responses to study guide items 6 to 8.

8. In Acts 27:42-44, how was Paul's life spared?

____

____

Why do you think the centurion felt as he did? _______________________

____

____

THE CONTINUING WITNESS

The promise given by God to Paul was fulfilled—all were ashore safely. Quickly, a curious crowd of the islanders gathered around the wet, shivering victims of the storm. A roaring fire was built. Luke calls these "barbarous people" (KJV) simply meaning that they were not Greeks.

9. **According to Acts 28:1,2, what island did they land on and how were they treated by the inhabitants?**

____

____

10. **Read Acts 28:3-6. What negative instance do we see occur fairly quickly, which God turns into a positive situation, not only for the benefit of those shipwrecked, but also for the furtherance of the gospel?**

____

The fatalistic view of these islanders provides interesting insight into heathenism. They apparently believed a number of things about sin. (1) Each individual is responsible for his/her own deeds. (2) A person's sins follow him/her and cry out for justice. (3) No one escapes the penalty of his/her sins. (4) The penalty of sin is death.

In their minds, Paul was probably guilty of some awful sin, such as murder. He had escaped death in the sea, but justice demanded punishment, hence, the waiting viper and the fatal snake bite.

The heathen knew that the wages of sin is death, but they did not know that the gift of God is eternal life through the Lord Jesus Christ. They knew the power of sin, but knew nothing of the power of redemption.

11. **Read Acts 28:7-10. What ministry opportunities opened to Paul as a result of his encounter by the fire?**

____

____

Paul, Luke, Aristarchus, and possibly the centurion Julius were included in this honor. For the next 3 months, as they waited for traveling weather, Paul preached, taught, and prayed for the sick. When the time came to leave the island, the people showered love gifts on Paul and his companions.

The long, arduous sea voyage ended at Puteoli. Almost immediately Paul was welcomed by believers who dwelt in this seaport. Just when this assembly of Christians was begun, and by whom, is not known. But the joy of Christian fellowship must have brought great blessing to Paul and his friends. They requested Paul to stay with them for 7 days, and, under one pretext or another, Julius permitted it. In the meanwhile, Julius sent word to Rome to notify the officials of his arrival and to request orders for the disposition of the prisoners.

12. Read Acts 28:11-16. Who met Paul at the Forum of Appius and the Three Taverns? What was Paul's reaction?

____

____

____

____

Some of the Roman Christians walked a distance of 40 miles. Others walked 30 miles to the Three Taverns. It was an amazing demonstration of love.

Without delay, Paul began his ministry in Rome. He was permitted to rent a private dwelling where he was detained under house arrest. Probably, he was in chains with a Roman soldier on guard at all times.

13. According to Acts 28:17-20, whom did Paul request to speak to and why?

____

____

____

14. According to Acts 28:21,22, what information had filtered to Rome concerning Paul?

____

____

____

They listened attentively as he spoke and testified of the kingdom of God. He spoke of Jesus using references from the law of Moses and from the Prophets.

15. Read Acts 28:23-25. What was the response of the Roman Jews?

____

____

____

16. Read Acts 28:26-28. On what did Paul decide to focus his attention concerning the Gentiles of Rome?

____

____

____

Distribute to each group member a copy of resource 13A, "A Time Line Of Paul." Point out the details of his ministry and how long he waited to fulfill his dream of reaching Rome.

Ask the following question: "What ministry dreams do you have?"

Encourage group members to spend a few moments in personal conversation with God, rededicating their God-given dreams.

Discussion
(2 minutes)

Ask group members, "Why does Paul always go to the Jews first even though they usually reject the message of Jesus?"

Response
(3 minutes)

Have group members share their responses to study guide item 14.

Now the full strength of Paul's energy was turned toward the Gentiles in Rome. He won converts from among the soldiers who were detailed to guard him. Men and women connected with the imperial palace came to the saving knowledge of Christ through Paul's unceasing witness. He sent greetings to the Philippian believers from the saints in Rome, identifying especially those from Caesar's household.

There is a marvelous passage in the letter Paul wrote to the church in Philippi which reflects his assessment of the sequence of events, all the way from the riot in the temple in Jerusalem to his present house arrest in Rome.

17. Look up Philippians 1:12-14. What kind of attitude did Paul have toward his persecution of the last couple of years?

____

____

Luke concludes the Book of Acts in what appears to be an abrupt stop. He leaves many questions unanswered. How we would like to know what happened when the 2-year period ended. Did Paul stand trial? Was he acquitted?

18. How does Luke end the Book of Acts? (Acts 28:30,31).

____

____

____

Many believe that Luke's final words about the continuation of Paul's ministry without hindrance mean that all charges against Paul were dropped because none of the Jews came to Rome to prosecute their complaints against him. And, with his release from house arrest, Paul was free to continue his ministry.

Several years before this, Paul had written to the Romans from the city of Corinth. He stated that he had a mission to perform in Jerusalem, and when this task was completed, he wanted to go to Spain, and en route he would come by Rome to minister there also (Romans 15:24-28).

Now, freed from the charges against him, was Paul able to fulfill his expressed wish to minister in Spain? This period of freedom did not extend beyond several years. The burning of Rome in A.D. 64 was blamed on the Christians and a fierce persecution was instigated against them. Once again Paul was apprehended, incarcerated this time in the Mamertine Prison, and eventually suffered martyrdom by order of Nero.

SUMMARY

Several years after the Titanic went down with terrible loss of life, a survivor stood in a testimony meeting to relate the unusual circumstance of his salvation. He told of drifting alone, clinging to a piece of wreckage, when John Harper of Glasgow drifted near him. "Man are you saved?" Harper asked. "No, I am not." "Believe on the Lord Jesus Christ and thou shalt be saved." A wave bore Harper away, but sometime later, the two men were near each other again. Once more Harper asked, "Are you saved now?" "No, I can't say I am." "Believe on the Lord Jesus Christ and thou shalt be saved." Not long after that Harper went down. "There alone, in the night, with 2 miles of water under me, I believed, and I knew that I was saved."

To Paul, every opportunity was precious, and none should be neglected. He was in chains, he was shipwrecked, went without food, despaired for his life, and was in a strange and foreign land, yet he took every opportunity to share Jesus with anyone he met. Paul did not let circumstances or personal discomfort deter him. The unresponsiveness of his audience did not force him to give up. He had fought a good fight; he had finished the course; he had kept the faith; and now a crown of righteousness awaited him.

LET'S REVIEW

1. What happened as the ship bearing Paul sailed to Phoenix for winter harbor?

____

____

2. What characteristic of Paul made an impact on the people traveling with him to Rome? How can you develop this characteristic?

____

____

____

____

3. What was the outcome of Paul's ministry on Malta?

____

____

____

4. Whom did Paul find when he landed at Puteoli?

____

____

5. How did the Roman believers manifest their love and concern for Paul?

____

____

____

6. Whom did Paul seek to reach first of all in Rome? With what success?

____

____

____

7. As a prisoner, how did Paul use his freedom to witness for Christ?

____

____

HOLY SPIRIT SURVEY

To assist the group leader in planning future sessions, please complete this survey to the best of your ability.

1. How do you feel about the use of all the gifts of the Spirit in today's Church?

2. Have you been baptized in the Holy Spirit?

3. If yes, when? Do you still have a fresh, on-going experience?

4. If no, are you interested in receiving the baptism in the Holy Spirit?

5. What do you hope to gain from this study?

The First Missionaries

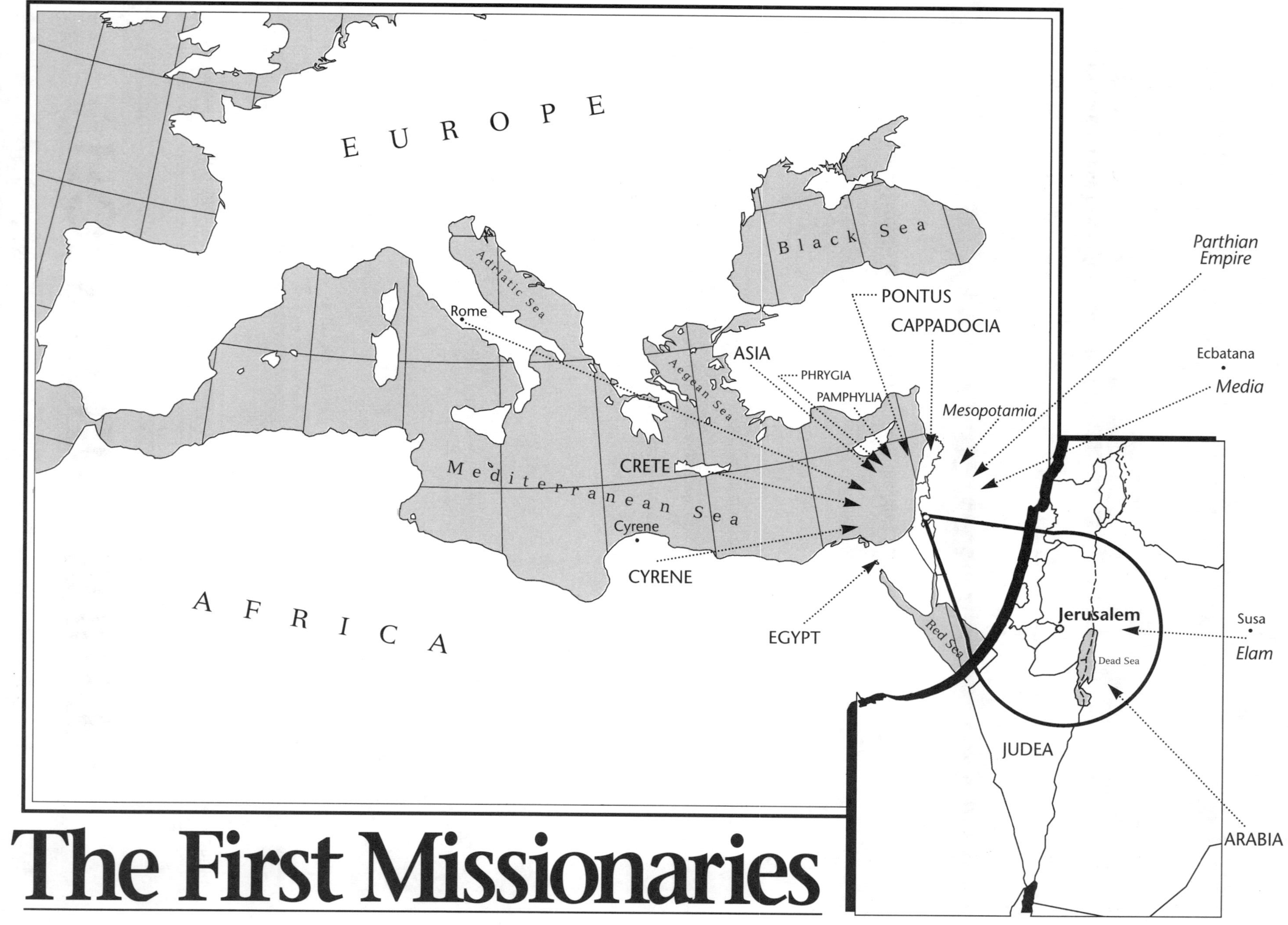

Resource 1B, *Acts: To The Ends Of The Earth*. Permission to reproduce this resource granted for local church use.
©1996 Gospel Publishing House

The Miracles Of The Apostles

Jesus promised the disciples they would perform mightier miracles then even He had after they received power from the Holy Spirit. A sampling of these miracles are recorded in the Book of Acts. Match the references listed below with the appropriate miracle.

____Acts 9:36-41	A. Lame man cured (by Peter)
____Acts 14:8-10	B. Healing of Publius' father
____Acts 3:6-9	C. Raising of Dorcas
____Acts 9:17,18	D. Demon cast out of a girl
____Acts 28:7-9	E. Raising of Eutychus
____Acts 5:1-10	F. Healing of Aeneas
____Acts 20:9,10	G. Death of Ananias and Sapphira
____Acts 9:33-35	H. Lame man cured (by Paul)
____Acts 28:3-5	I. Elymas blinded
____Acts 13:8-11	J. Paul unharmed by viper
____Acts 16:16-18	K. Saul's sight restored

How Can We Witness?

As we have seen, the Book of Acts presents several examples of witnessing. There are different methods to show to the world a witness of Jesus Christ. Each is vital to our overall witness to our world. In which of these ways have you witnessed? What are some practical examples of ways you have witnessed, or seen others witness, to the power of the resurrection using these five categories?

Witness Through Preaching

Witness Through Baptism

Witness Through Fellowship

Witness Through Miracle Power

Witness Through Assurance

Saddu-who?

In the years surrounding the life of Jesus, two parties formed in the Jewish religion—the Pharisees and the Sadducees. It is important to understand their background and beliefs when reading the Bible, as both groups played a large part in the development of the Early Church. These two pages offer a brief history of the Sadducees and Pharisees.

The Sadducees

<u>Name</u>

Sadducees has three possible translations:
1. "the Righteous Ones"—based on the Hebrew consonants for the word *righteous*
2. "ones who sympathize with Zadok," or "Zadokites"—based on their possible link to Zadok the high priest
3. "syndics," "judges," or "fiscal controllers"—based on the greek word *syndikoi*

<u>Origin and existence</u>

✦ Unknown origin though they claimed to be descendants of Zadok—high priest under David (see 2 Samuel 8:17; 15:24) and Solomon (see 1 Kings 1:34,35; 1 Chronicles 12:28)
✦ Had a possible link to Aaron
✦ Were probably formed into a group about 200 B.C. as the high priest's party
✦ Aristocracy—the rich descendants of the high-priestly line (However, not all priests were Sadducees.)
✦ Demise in A.D. 70 with the destruction of the temple

<u>Beliefs</u>

✦ Probably accepted only the *Torah* (Genesis through Deuteronomy) as authoritative
✦ Practiced literal interpretation of the Law
✦ Rigidly conservative towards the Law
✦ Stressed strict observance of the Law
✦ Observed past beliefs and tradition
✦ Opposed oral law as obligatory or binding
✦ Believed in the absolute freedom of the human will—that people could do as they wished without attention from God
✦ Denied divine providence
✦ Denied the concept of life after death and the resurrection of the body
✦ Denied the concept of reward and punishment after death
✦ Denied the existence of angels and demons
✦ Materialistic

<u>What does the Bible say about them?</u>

2 Samuel 8:17; 15:24; 1 Kings 1:34; 1 Chronicles 12:26-28; Ezekiel 40:45,46; 43:19; 44:15,16; Matthew 3:7-10; 16:1,6-12; 22:23-34; Mark 12:18-27; Luke 20:27-40; John 11:47; Acts 4:1,2; 5:17,18; 23:6-10

<u>Activities</u>

✦ In charge of the temple and its services
✦ Politically active
✦ Exercised great political control through the Sanhedrin of which many were members
✦ Supported the ruling power and the status quo
✦ Leaned toward Hellenism (the spreading of Greek influence) and were therefore despised by the Jewish populace
✦ Opposed both the Pharisees and Jesus because these lived by the larger canon (The Pharisees and Jesus both considered more than only Genesis through Deuteronomy as authoritative.)
✦ Opposed Jesus specifically for fear their wealth/position would be threatened if they supported Him

The Pharisees

<u>Name</u>

Pharisees translates "the Separated Ones" with three possible meanings:
1. to their separating themselves from people
2. to their separating themselves to the study of the Law
3. to their separating themselves from pagan practices

<u>**Origin and existence**</u>

◆ Originated approximately 160 B.C.
◆ Most numerous of the Jewish parties (but still not very large)
◆ Probably spiritual descendants of the Hasidim (religious freedom fighters)—scribes and lawyers
◆ Members of the middle class—mostly businessmen (merchants and tradesmen)

<u>**Beliefs**</u>

◆ Monotheistic
◆ Viewed entirety of the Old Testament (Law, Prophets, and Writings) as authoritative
◆ Believed that the study of the Law was true worship
◆ Accepted both the written and oral law
◆ More liberal in interpreting the Law than were the Sadducees
◆ Quite concerned with the proper keeping of the Sabbath, tithing, and purification rituals
◆ Believed in life after death and the resurrection of the body (with divine retribution and reward)
◆ Believed in the reality of demons and angels
◆ Revered humanity and human equality
◆ Missionary-minded regarding the conversion of Gentiles
◆ Believed that individuals were responsible for how they lived

<u>**What does the Bible say about them?**</u>

Matthew 3:7-10; 5:20; 9:14; 16:1,6-12; 22:15-22, 34-46; 23:2-36; Mark 2:16; 3:6; 7:3-5; 8:15; 12:13-17; Luke 5:17,21; 6:7; 7:36-39; 11:37-44; 18:9-14; John 3:1,2; 9:13-16; 11:46,47; 12:19; Acts 23:6-10; Philippians 3:4-6

<u>**Activities**</u>

◆ Developers of oral tradition
◆ Taught that the way to God was through obedience to the Law
◆ Changed Judaism from a religion of sacrifice to a religion of law
◆ Progressive thinkers regarding the adaptation of the Law to new situations
◆ Opposed Jesus because He would not accept the teachings of the oral law as binding
◆ Established and controlled synagogues
◆ Exercised great control over general population
◆ Served as religious authorities for most Jews
◆ Took several ceremonies from the temple to the home
◆ Emphasized ethical as opposed to theological action
◆ Legalistic and socially exclusive (shunned non-Pharisees as unclean)
◆ Tended to have a self-sufficient and haughty attitude

Whom Should I Tell?

Every conversion is a miracle filled with eternal meaning. A Sunday School teacher, Edward Kimball, stood outside Samuel Holton's shoe store in Boston. It was a beautiful May day in the year 1856. Inside the store was a young man about whom the Sunday School teacher was greatly concerned. The young man was employed by his uncle as a shoe clerk and part of the condition of his employment was the promise that he would attend church and Sunday School.

The teacher, learning that the young man was not converted, had come determined to speak to him about Christ. With courage born of the Spirit, Kimball entered the store and discovered that his pupil was in the back room, quite alone, wrapping shoes. Kimball went to him, put his hand on his shoulder, and told him of Christ's love and of the love Jesus wanted in return. It was a simple, beautiful moment. The young shoe clerk, Dwight L. Moody, surrendered his life to Jesus Christ, and from that instant, became a witness for his Lord. Kimball had no way of knowing that this young shoe clerk was destined to lay hold of America and England and move the English-speaking world toward God.

Qualifications For A Missionary

What does it take to be a missionary? J. Hudson Taylor, founder of the China Inland Mission, gave a description of necessary missionary qualities. He said missionary candidates need the following attributes:

1. A life yielded to God and controlled by His Spirit.

2. A restful trust in God for the supply of all needs.

3. A sympathetic spirit and a willingness to take a lowly place.

4. Tact in dealing with people.

5. Adaptability toward circumstances.

6. Zeal in service and steadfastness in discouragement.

7. Love for communion with God and for the study of His Word.

Effective Evangelism

Effective evangelism doesn't just happen. There are several factors which must exist before a soul winner can be used of God in leading someone to Christ. The account of Philip and the Ethiopian presents several of these factors.

1. All who live and move in the Spirit may expect God's direction.

   An angel gave Philip clear instructions about where to go and to whom to speak.

2. The soul winner must yield unquestioningly and immediately.

   Philip could have used many reasonable excuses for questioning the guidance to Gaza.

3. God brings people together with perfect timing.

   Philip and the Ethiopian were drawn together at just the right moment.

4. God will reveal the approach to each person's soul.

   The Ethiopian was already seeking God. His question gave Philip the opportunity to share.

5. It is essential to have a working knowledge of God's Word.

   Philip knew the passage the Ethiopian was struggling to understand and was therefore able to explain it to him.

6. Ultimately, Christ as Savior is your all-sufficient message.

   Philip shared the message of Christ's salvation with the Ethiopian.

Dealing With Difficult Situations

Some things in life just do not make sense to us humans. Why does an innocent child have to deal with the pain of cancer while a mass murderer lives to a ripe old age in prison? Why is one healed and not another? Why are some Christians blessed with freedom of religion while others must endure the persecution of unsympathetic government officials? These are situations that don't seem to meet with our sense of justice and can cause discontentment and anger.

So, how can we reconcile these apparent imbalances? God understands our questions and the Bible presents information we can use to help us gain understanding and peace. Read each of the Scripture references given below and summarize the perspective given in each passage.

Job 1:21,22 ____

Job 12:13 ____

Job 13:15 ____

Psalm 73:21-26 ____

Ecclesiastes 3:11 ____

Ecclesiastes 7:13,14 ____

Isaiah 40:13,14 ____

Isaiah 43:2 ____

Daniel 3:16-18 ____

Habakkuk 3:17-19 ____

Matthew 5:44,45 ____

Matthew 10:16-31 ____

Romans 5:1-5____

Romans 8:22,23,28 ____

Romans 11:33 ____

1 Corinthians 15:54-57 ____

2 Corinthians 1:3,4 ____

2 Corinthians 4:8,9,16-18 ____

2 Corinthians 12:7-10 ____

Philippians 4:6,7,11-13 ____

1 Thessalonians 5:16-18 ____

Hebrews 2:17,18 ____

Hebrews 5:8 ____

Hebrews 11:32-40 ____

James 1:3 ____

1 Peter 4:12-19 ____

1 Peter 5:10 ____

LABORERS TOGETHER

At a biennial meeting of her denomination, Miss Lillian Trasher publicly gave thanks to all who had assisted her in the great work of the orphanage in Assiout, Egypt. For over 50 years Miss Trasher had given of herself in ministry to the children and widows of Egypt. Scarcely ever were there less than 1,000 children in the orphanage to feed and clothe and educate.

As Miss Trasher stood to speak, she turned to ask Mrs. Marie Brown, of Glad Tidings Tabernacle, New York City, to come and stand by her side. Miss Trasher related how in the goodness of God, she had been led to Glad Tidings Tabernacle when she first went to Egypt. At that time she was unknown and without the support of a church. Pastor and Mrs. Robert Brown received her and pledged support for her work. With tears, Miss Trasher said, "For the past 50 years, never failing once, each month an offering from Glad Tidings has come to strengthen and assist the work of the orphanage. For this I give thanks to God, to the congregation, and to dear Sister Brown!" And while these two precious servants of God embraced, the entire congregation at that meeting joined them in praise to God.

What a beautiful example of what it means to be "laborers together with God." Not all are called or able to "go," but we are all called of God to work for His kingdom in whatever capacity possible. Some will go; some will stay. Some physically take the message of salvation. Some send these out with financial help. Some supply goods and materials for ministry. Some send up prayers for protection and guidance. Some raise up new missionaries through spiritual guidance and education. But in the end, we have all been called in some way to be involved in fulfilling the Great Commission. It is our responsibility to our Lord to do what He asks us to do so that every area of ministry is covered.

Paul's Journeys

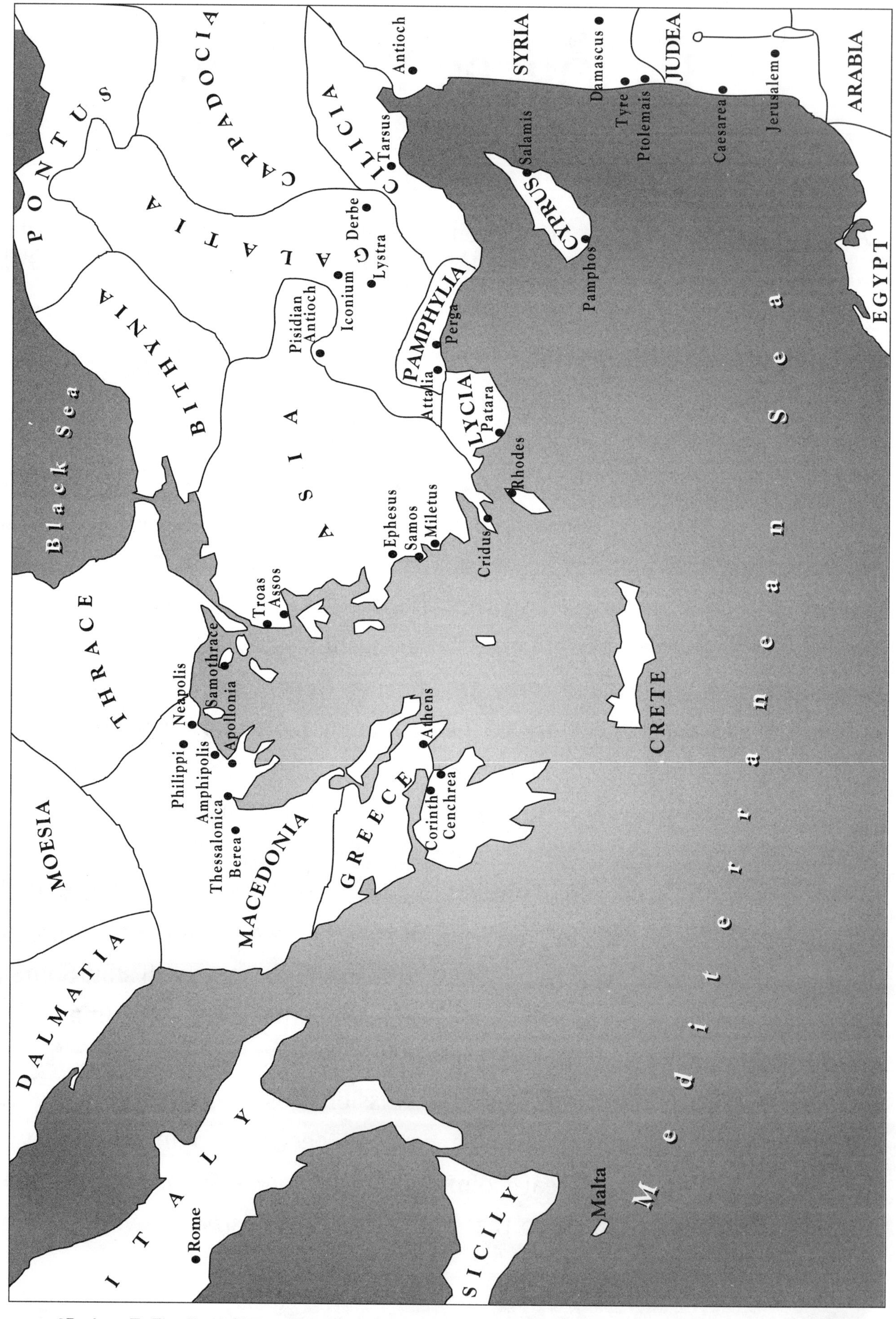

Resource 6B, *Acts: To The Ends Of The Earth.* Permission to reproduce this resource granted for local church use.
©1996 Gospel Publishing House

Which Way Is Right?

Each year several thousand people converge upon a small town in the midwest portion of the United States of America for a 4-day Christian concert. They come to hear Christian musicians and speakers. Some just come to relax and camp and enjoy the camaraderie of Christian fellowship. The music and seminars cover a wide range of interests; therefore the attendees reflect this variety.

A pastor and his wife, from the area of the concert site, received complimentary passes to attend the concert. As they walked through the tents and trailers of the many campers, they came upon a small outdoor platform. The young people performing at this stage looked like a band one might expect to see involved in secular music. The crowd included individuals with dyed hair, ear and nose rings. The music consisted of high decibel guitar riffs and loud vocals. Despite their initial distaste for the musical style, the pastor and his wife stopped to listen and observe. As they watched, the words of the band's song became clear. The essence was this, "God, Almighty, loves *me*. I love Him. I am singing this song because I love Him so much and I want Him and everyone else to know."

That pastor and his wife learned something that day. In spite of their obvious differences, these young people and they had something deeper in common—the love of Jesus Christ and a return of that love. They were both interested in sharing that love with the people around them—only their methods differed.

1. Personal appearance and expression are often dividers of people. In what other areas do we impose our "religious" rules on the people who come into our churches? (new converts, visitors, or people with unique ministry ideas)

2. How can we avoid placing these restrictions on others and build a community of love and acceptance?

Facing The Issue

Jewish Questions	**Christianity's Response**
1. God had chosen Israel, and the physical sign of that covenant was circumcision. Had God's Law been nullified? Had He changed His mind?	1. Yes. God spoke to the fathers through Israel's prophets, but now He has spoken to us through His Son. The Lord Jesus Christ is superior in position and authority to any of the servants or covenants in Israel's past.
2. Jesus himself was a Jew and had submitted to the Law. Should His followers do less?	2. True, Jesus submitted to all the demands of the Law. But He himself stated that He had come to fulfill the Law (Matthew 5:17).
3. All the promises of redemption, including the Messiah, had come through Israel. Could individuals turn away from Israel and the promises of God and still claim the redemption those promises offered?	3. Yes. The covenants and promises of Israel pointed to Christ and were fulfilled in Him. When we receive Jesus all these are embraced and are validated in our relationship with Him.
4. Circumcision, in a sense, was like taking the cross to follow Jesus. It was part of the price that must be paid. Were they unwilling to pay the price?	4. There is no objection to the act of circumcision except as it is offered as a means of salvation. To argue that circumcision was essential, weakens and corrupts the gospel of grace.

Tentmaking Today

In Acts 18:1-3, Luke relates that Paul worked with Aquila and Priscilla because they were all tentmakers. To this point it has not been mentioned that Paul had to support himself while ministering, but this passage shows he is willing to do whatever is necessary to further the spread of the gospel.

The traditional missionary today is sent out to the mission field with the financial support of churches and individuals so that ministry is the primary concern of that individual. More recently the term tentmaker has been employed to identify the growing number of Christians who live and work overseas (and in their home country) under nonreligious conditions, for the sole purpose of using their secular job as an opportunity to give witness of Jesus Christ.

Tentmaking is a new twist in world evangelism. Some countries do not allow traditional missionaries to enter their borders due to political or religious alignment. But most welcome with open arms an individual who is willing to come work in the business and industry of their country. English is emerging as an almost worldwide language, spoken by approximately one-fifth of the world's population. Because of this, English teachers are in demand in many countries and communication is becoming more universal.

There are several opportunities for modern tentmakers. One possibility is to teach in government schools or secular universities. In this way individuals are recognized as missionaries but are paid by the government of the country in which they are working. These teaching positions may include basic courses or even classes on religion. And because the resident country knows the tentmaker is a Christian, there is nothing to hide. What an opportunity!

Other host countries will not allow open witnessing but appreciate the willingness of foreigners to work and learn with them. In these situations, the tentmakers must walk a tightrope. They are under close surveillance and sometimes are prohibited from establishing friendly relations with people.

One growing method of tentmaking is students who attend foreign universities. These tentmakers take a year or two of studies in a foreign country. Once again, this opportunity is open to many individuals where traditional missionary endeavors are not possible. Many universities are more than happy to have foreign students attend as it lends credibility to their programs.

Another tentmaking possibility involves postretirement individuals. Their financial independence, maturity, experience, and dependability make them attractive both to missions boards and government officials. Some opportunities open to them are teaching positions at national or missionary children schools, host/hostess at mission homes, assisting with office work at mission field offices, and assisting with general maintenance and construction jobs. With their experience, they can help with almost anything.

There are also many short-term opportunities. These are perhaps more like traditional missions work in that the workers usually raise support to fund their work and often work with a traditional missionary when they arrive at their host country. One possibility in this area is a summer internship for students either working in their field of study or just helping out where they can. Another opportunity is a 2- or 3-week assignment to assist in churches, offices, or as a construction team.

There is one thing to remember. Regardless of the methods, the missionary movement will continue to the end of the age (Mark 13:10). The missions endeavor is God's, not man's, and He is perfectly able to take care of His business. God is in control and the missionary movement is in His plan for world evangelization.

Ephesus Fact Sheet

During the time of Paul, perhaps only Corinth rivaled Ephesus for its level of debauchery. The two cities were closely related due to the trade routes that made their way through both cities. These trade routes included sea to the west and land to the east. Ephesus was known as the "metropolis of Asia," the meeting place of East and West. Among Eastern cities, Ephesus was only second in size to Alexandria. It was the capital of proconsular Asia and a governor resided there.

Its Temple of Artemis (Diana) was one of the seven wonders of the ancient world. According to ancient writers who had seen the Hanging Gardens of Babylon, the Colossus of Rhodes, and the pyramids of Egypt, none compared to the Temple of Artemis. It has been called the most impressive structure ever built. Measuring 418 feet long by 239 feet wide, it had 117 columns, each 60 feet high, and each a gift from a king. This temple also served as a sanctuary providing refuge and right of asylum.

Ephesus spawned the first bank—the Temple of Artemis made loans with the large offerings given by the many who visited it. It brimmed with Roman power and splendor; some of its streets were paved with marble. On the western slope of the city the Greeks had built one of their largest amphitheaters, with a seating capacity of over 24,000 people. It was truly a great city and one Paul wanted to reach with the gospel.

Ephesus was a melting pot of cultures, religions, and races. Along with the worship of Artemis, the use of magic was highly prevalent, so much so, ancient Greek and Roman writers identified books of incantations and magical formulas as "Ephesian writings." This acceptance of many religions was both positive and negative for the new Christian Church. It was positive in the sense that it did not initially arouse much animosity in the city leaders. It was negative because of the danger of the new believers continuing this religious acceptance and bringing heathen practices into the Church.

The church planted in Ephesus through the labors of Paul was only one of a circuit that were planted. The spread of the gospel was helped by the city's central location and the ease of travel. Seven of these churches were the recipients of the letters from Patmos as given to John and recorded in Revelation. Both John and Luke spent their later years in Ephesus.

Bringing It Home

The apostle Paul was a man of strong conviction and commitment. God had called him to preach the gospel and preach he did. When difficulties arose he took them in stride as a part of God's overall plan for salvation of the human race. He never gave up. Consider the following and record your responses.

1. List some modern-day "Pauls" you have known or heard about. Describe the situation which confronted these individuals.

2. In what day-to-day situations in your own life could you be a "Paul" to the people around you? In what ways would you be willing to do more to share the gospel of Christ?

Holy Ground

Below are two records that demonstrate the extent to which Jews uphold the sacredness of the temple of God. Read them and then answer the following question.

In 1871, there was discovered in Jerusalem a limestone block 23 inches high, 34 inches long, and 15 inches thick. It is now on display in an Istanbul museum. Cut deeply into the stone is an inscription which has been translated: "No foreigner may enter within the railing or boundary line of the sanctuary. Whoever is caught is himself responsible for the consequence, which is death."

The violent differences between Jewish parties did not die with the Sadducees and Pharisees. In recent history, the entire city of Jerusalem has again returned to Israeli control. Perhaps one of the most revered shrines in Israel is the Western Wall, also called the Wailing Wall. It is all that remains of an ancient wall around the temple area. Since the Six Day War in 1967, the area has been cleared and beautifully lighted. Praying Jews may be seen leaning against it, or bobbing their heads in meditation and prayer before the Wall at any time of day or night.

Ultraconservative Jews felt at that time that the liberal Jews would defile this place with their unbelief in the Scriptures. Bitter debate about who should be permitted to worship at the Western Wall caused sharp feelings. Conservatives threatened a blood bath if the Liberals tried to hold services at the Wall. The Liberals ridiculed such acrimonious feelings. "Why all this excitement?" they asked. "After all, the area near the Western Wall is only the street outside the temple area. It is not holy ground!"

In light of this emotional intensity toward the holiness of the temple, why do you suppose Paul began his defense by stating he was a Jew? (Acts 22:3-21).

Sacrilege!

You have been wrongfully accused of religious sacrilege—violating something that is considered sacred. Your life is being threatened and you are your only defense. Write below how you would present a defense to the local court hearing your case. Remember, the court may not accept your belief system at its face value.

Paul's Defense

The Charges

1. An instigator of a revolt against Rome; a plague; a public nuisance.

(An attempt by the accusers to influence Felix after praising him for his peacekeeping efforts.)

2. An enemy of Israel as the ringleader of the Nazarene sect.

(An attempt to turn the Romans against the Christians and dissociate Christians from any relationship with Judaism.)

3. A desecrater of the temple; had also profaned the holy place.

(Even the Romans recognized the sacredness of the temple and any offense against it was considered a serious outrage by the Roman court.)

The Defense

1. The charge of insurrection was ridiculous. He had only been in Jerusalem a few days and he had not been found in public or private debate.

2. Yes, he was a follower of "the Way." Christianity was the fulfillment of the promises of God to the fathers of Israel. How can that be heresy?

3. He absolutely did not desecrate the temple! He was fulfilling holy vows when Asian Jews assaulted him. They had desecrated the temple. And where were his accusers? Did he not have a right to face them?

A Time Line Of Paul

A.D. 5 —— BIRTH OF SAUL (BETWEEN 6 B.C. AND A.D. 10, BUT PROBABLY ABOUT A.D. 5)

35 MARTYRDOM OF STEPHEN (ACTS 7:57-60)
35 CONVERSION OF SAUL (ACTS 9:1-19)

35-38 ARABIAN TRIP (GALATIANS 1:17) FITS IN AT ACTS 9:23 DURING THE "MANY DAYS"

38 TWO-WEEK VISIT TO JERUSALEM (ACTS 9:26-29; GALATIANS 1:18,19)

38-43 MINISTRY IN SYRIA AND CILICIA (ACTS 9:30; GALATIANS 1:21)

43 ARRIVAL IN SYRIAN ANTIOCH (ACTS 11:25,26)

43-44 FAMINE VISIT (ACTS 11:27-30; 12:25)

46-48 FIRST MISSIONARY JOURNEY (ACTS 13:2 TO 14:28)

49-50 JERUSALEM CONFERENCE (ACTS 15:1-29; GALATIANS 2:1-10?)

50-52 SECOND MISSIONARY JOURNEY (ACTS 15:40 TO 18:23)

51-52 APPEARANCE BEFORE GALLIO (ACTS 18:12-17)

52 RETURN TO JERUSALEM AND SYRIAN ANTIOCH (ACTS 18:22)

53-57 THIRD MISSIONARY JOURNEY (ACTS 18:23 TO 21:17)

53-55 AT EPHESUS (ACTS 19:1 TO 20:1)

57 ARREST IN JERUSALEM (ACTS 21:27 TO 22:30)

57-59 CAESAREAN IMPRISONMENT (ACTS 23:23 TO 26:32)

59 SHIPWRECK VOYAGE TO ROME (ACTS 27:1 TO 28:16)

59-61/62 FIRST ROMAN IMPRISONMENT (ACTS 28:16-31)

62 RELEASE FROM ROMAN PRISON

62-67 FOURTH MISSIONARY JOURNEY INCLUDING MINISTRY ON CRETE (TITUS 1:5)

67-68 SECOND ROMAN IMPRISONMENT (2 TIMOTHY 4:6-8) TRIAL AND EXECUTION

Acts: To The Ends Of The Earth Evaluation

Please complete this form and return it to the publisher. We are interested in your opinion of our curricular material. We will use your insights and suggestions as we develop additional titles in the *Spiritual Discovery Series*. We would be interested in hearing from you whether you have positive comments or negative. The editorial staff of the *Spiritual Discovery Series* wish to develop a product that ministers to the needs of our users. Thank you in advance for taking a few moments to complete this evaluation.

1. In what study setting was the title *Acts: To The Ends Of The Earth* used?

_____ Individual   _____ Home Fellowship   _____ Sunday School   _____ Other:______________________________

2. What was your initial reaction to the following?

	Excellent	Good	Poor
Cover Art	_____	_____	_____
Appearance Of Inside Text	_____	_____	_____
Size Of The Leader's Guide	_____	_____	_____
Size Of The Study Guide	_____	_____	_____
3-Hole Punched Leader's Guide	_____	_____	_____
Perforation Of Leader's Guide	_____	_____	_____
Price Of Leader's Guide	_____	_____	_____

3. How do you evaluate the usefulness of the following?

	Excellent	Good	Poor
3-Hole Punched Leader's Guide	_____	_____	_____
Perforation Of Leader's Guide	_____	_____	_____
Leader's Methodology	_____	_____	_____
Resource Pages	_____	_____	_____
Study Guide Text In Leader's Guide	_____	_____	_____

4. How effective were the following elements of the curriculum?

	Excellent	Good	Poor
Study Objectives	_____	_____	_____
Getting The Group's Attention	_____	_____	_____
Transition Statements	_____	_____	_____
Methodology	_____	_____	_____
Let's Review	_____	_____	_____
Resource Pages	_____	_____	_____
Study Guide Material	_____	_____	_____

5. On a scale of 1 to 5 (5 being excellent), how do you rate the "user friendliness" of the product? ______________________

6. Did most group members complete the study guide material before they arrived at the session? ____________________

7. Did group members actively participate in group sessions? ____________________

8. What was the most useful element of the product?

9. How would you improve the product to make it more useful for the leader?

10. Additional Comments: